ANDREW QAPPIK
Pangnirtung Memories

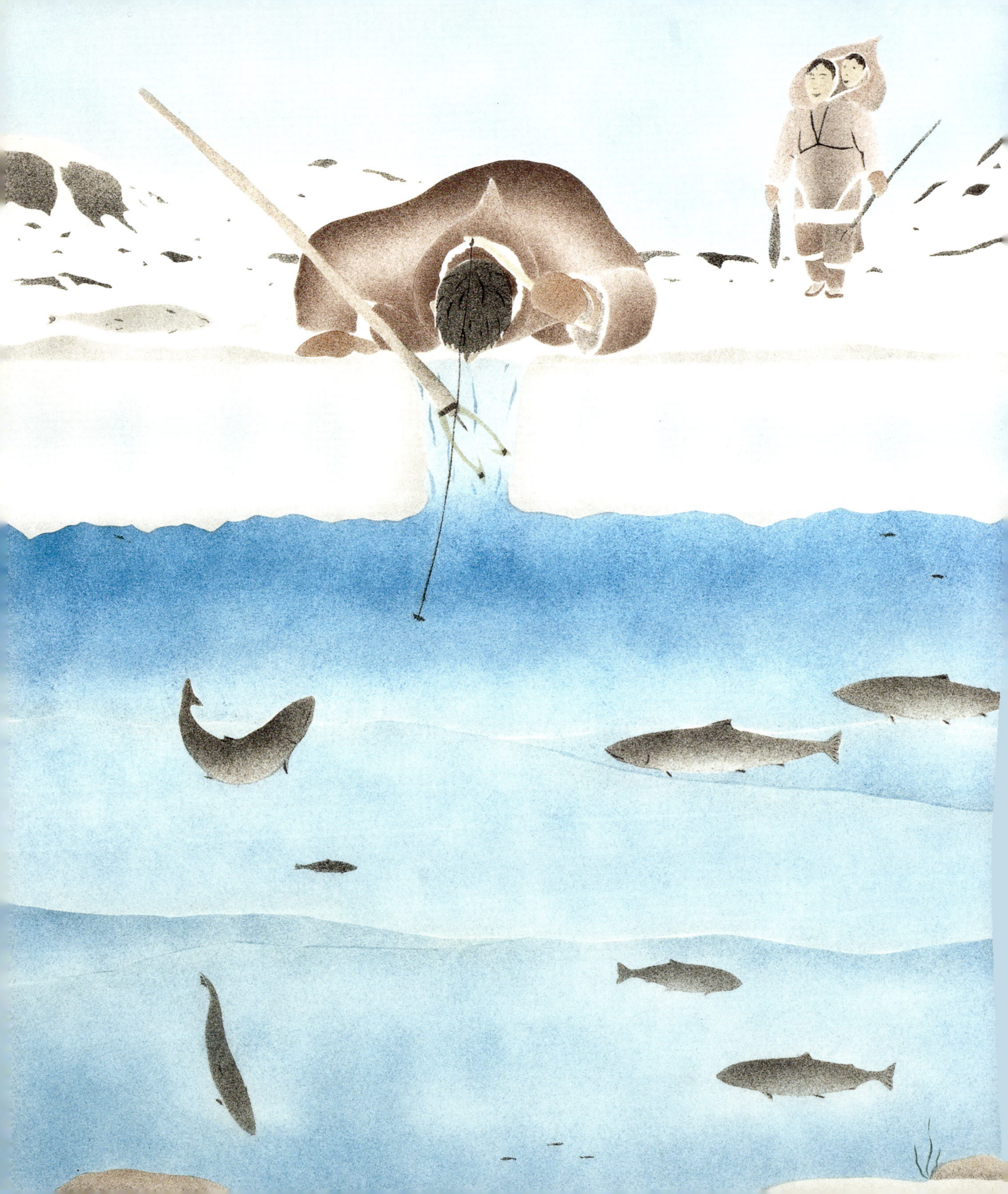

ANDREW QAPPIK
Pangnirtung Memories

Curated by Darlene Coward Wight
Essays by H.G. Jones and Darlene Coward Wight

Winnipeg Art Gallery
2010

wag

Andrew Qappik: Pangnirtung Memories

Library and Archives Canada Cataloguing in Publication

Wight, Darlene

Andrew Qappik : Pangnirtung memories / curated by

Darlene Coward Wight ; essays by H.G. Jones and Darlene Coward Wight.
Includes bibliographical references.

Catalogue of an exhibition held at the Winnipeg Art Gallery from April 29–Aug. 1, 2010.

ISBN 978-0-88915-005-8

1. Qappik, Andrew, 1964- --Exhibitions. I. Qappik, Andrew, 1964-
II. Jones, H. G. (Houston Gwynne), 1924 III. Winnipeg Art Gallery IV. Title.

NE542.3.Q36A4 2010 769.92 C2010-902895-3

Artwork on page ii: *Favourite Place to Be*, 1993

CREDITS
Photographer: Ernest Mayer (painting), Leif Norman (prints)
Designer: Lisa Friesen
Copy Editor: Joan Padgett
Proofreader: Heather Mousseau
Printer: Friesens Corporation

Printed and bound in Canada
Distribution: ABC Art Books Canada, www.ABCartbookscanada.com
All works are in the collection of the Winnipeg Art Gallery

Exhibition sponsored by The Dorothy Strelsin Foundation and First Air

Winnipeg Art Gallery • wag.ca

Contents

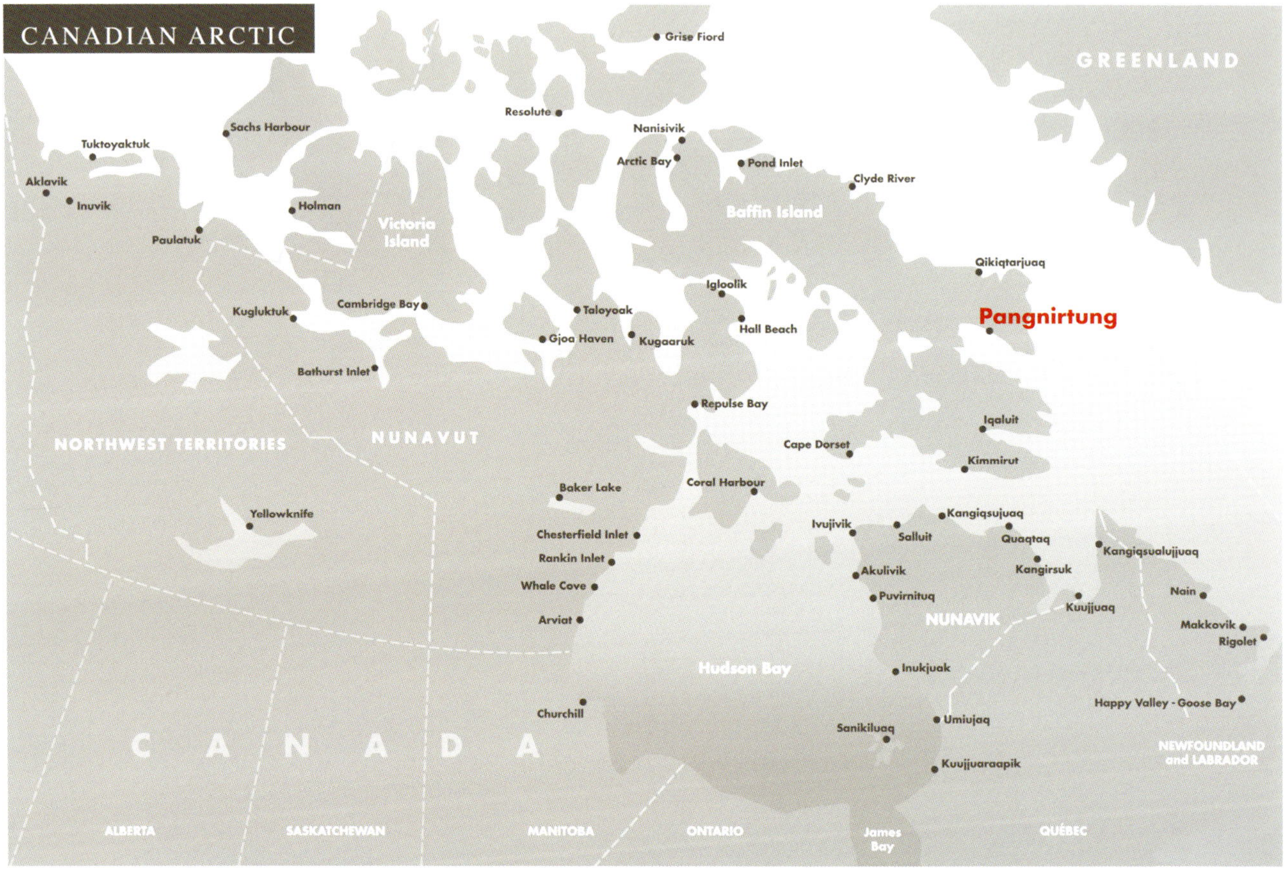
CANADIAN ARCTIC
GREENLAND
Grise Fiord
Resolute
Sachs Harbour
Nanisivik
Arctic Bay
Pond Inlet
Clyde River
Tuktoyaktuk
Aklavik
Inuvik
Holman
Paulatuk
Victoria Island
Baffin Island
Qikiqtarjuaq
Igloolik
Pangnirtung
Kugluktuk
Cambridge Bay
Taloyoak
Hall Beach
Gjoa Haven
Kugaaruk
Bathurst Inlet
Repulse Bay
Iqaluit
NORTHWEST TERRITORIES
NUNAVUT
Cape Dorset
Kimmirut
Baker Lake
Coral Harbour
Yellowknife
Ivujivik
Kangiqsujuaq
Salluit
Chesterfield Inlet
Quaqtaq
Kangiqsualujjuaq
Rankin Inlet
Akulivik
Kangirsuk
Whale Cove
Puvirnituq
Nain
Kuujjuaq
Arviat
NUNAVIK
Makkovik
Rigolet
Hudson Bay
Inukjuak
Churchill
Happy Valley - Goose Bay
Umiujaq
Sanikiluaq
C A N A D A
NEWFOUNDLAND and LABRADOR
Kuujjuaraapik
ALBERTA
SASKATCHEWAN
MANITOBA
ONTARIO
James Bay
QUÉBEC

Preface

The Winnipeg Art Gallery is pleased to present the first solo retrospective exhibition of work by Andrew Qappik, a talented artist from Pangnirtung on east Baffin Island. Over the years, the Gallery has presented a number of exhibitions that focus on the work of individual Inuit artists who express their visual and cultural concerns in various two- and three-dimensional media. Qappik is a graphic artist who has created drawings since the age of five. From 1978 to the present he has mastered the printing techniques of stonecut, stencil, etching, and lithography to interpret his drawings. Most recently he has been exploring the medium of oil paint, and one work in oil created in 2009 is included in the exhibition.

The exhibition also honours the recent donation to the Gallery of all Andrew Qappik's limited-edition prints by collector Dr. H.G. Jones. Dr. Jones is Professor Emeritus of History, University of North Carolina at Chapel Hill. Although his area of expertise in his professional career has been researching the history of North Carolina, he has spent over 35 years travelling to the Canadian Arctic and studying Inuit history and culture. He began to collect Qappik's prints in 1978 and usually made annual trips to Pangnirtung to purchase prints and lend his encouragement to the artist. His written contribution to this catalogue gives insights into a special relationship between artist and collector. We would also like to thank the Council for Canadian American Relations for facilitating this donation. This organization allows citizens of the United States to receive tax advantages for contributions of art to Canadian institutions.

The WAG's collection of Inuit art has been largely formed by the vision of collectors such as Dr. Jones. They have supported the work of artists through their purchases and have supported the Gallery through their donations. The sponsors of our exhibitions play an important role as well, and I would like to thank The Dorothy Strelsin Foundation for its long-time support of the Gallery's Inuit and contemporary exhibitions. The artist's travel to the Gallery was made possible by First Air. Lastly, I would like to thank WAG Curator of Inuit Art, Darlene Coward Wight, for organizing this exhibition and preparing the catalogue.

Stephen Borys, PhD, MBA
Director, Winnipeg Art Gallery

Andrew Qappik: A Collector's Perspective

H.G. Jones

My first visit to Pangnirtung coincided in 1972 with that Inuit community's experimentation in printmaking. The following year, the first catalogued collection of Pangnirtung prints was released. In the local co-operative, I watched two of the printmakers, Imoona Karpik and Solomon Karpik, as they turned original drawings into handsome stencil and stonecut images. Usually hanging around them was their eight-year-old nephew Andrew Karpik. On subsequent visits I was impressed by the intensity with which the youngster watched the older printmakers, often drawing and experimenting himself. Still, I was not prepared when the 1978 Pangnirtung print collection included five of Andrew's own drawings. Art advisor John Houston commented in the preface, "...we are expecting more interesting images from him." In thirty-two years, Andrew—who changed the spelling of his surname to Qappik in 1994—has disappointed neither Houston nor other Inuit art enthusiasts.

Having more interest in the boy prodigy than in the art itself, I purchased all of Andrew's first-year prints. The 1979 catalogue included four of his drawings, and the next year, two. Remarkably, the youngster had produced 11 prints by age 16—all without a day of formal artistic instruction. I became so obsessed with acquiring all of the youth's prints that I arranged to have them shipped to me if I failed to get to Baffin Island in a particular year. That's why the Winnipeg Art Gallery now has the only comprehensive set of Andrew Qappik's prints.

Over three decades I have had the pleasure of seeing the young man develop into a fine artist. In addition to producing prints, he has illustrated several elementary school textbooks published in Inuktitut, drawn colourful posters for the Canadian Coast Guard, furnished drawings from which handsome tapestries have been made in the Pangnirtung Tapestry Studio, carved and painted wooden signs for entrepreneurs and government agencies, designed a coin for the Royal Canadian Mint, and—most significant of all—designed both the coat of arms and the flag of the new territory of Nunavut, formed from the Northwest Territories in 1999.

Having been born on the land, Andrew Qappik has a special affinity with the traditional Inuit way of subsistence—following wildlife and surviving on what nature provides. His maternal grandfather Eliyah Keenainak often took him hunting and whaling, so many of Andrew's prints capture images of the "old ways." At age 20 Andrew said, "The drawings I do are for the people who suffered and who struggled for their lives—for food and clothing. What strength was used by our great-grandfathers in their livelihood." Not surprisingly, many of his prints depict that struggle.

Andrew's deep respect for animal life is reflected in his touching scenes of polar bears and their cubs. Traditionally, Inuit believe that an animal sacrifices itself for human consumption because, when shown proper respect and ritual (for example, squirting fresh water into the mouth of a newly killed seal), its spirit will be reborn in another. Andrew's consciousness of tradition is also reflected in Inuit legends, such as those related to the sea spirit, Talilajuq (also Sedna or Nuliajuk). Remembering being carried in his family's *umiak*

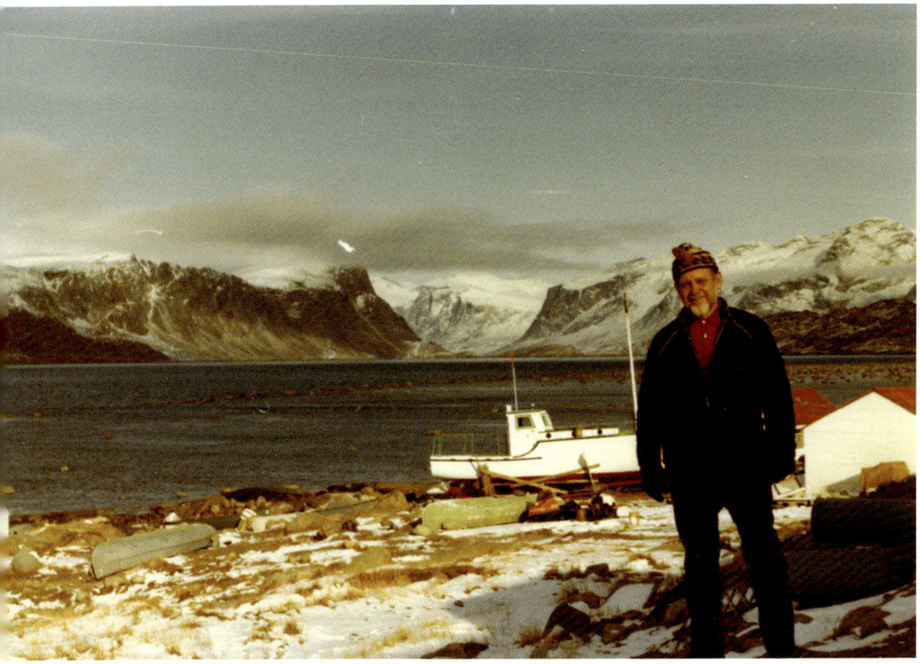

H.G. Jones in Pangnirtung, 1970s. Photo by Harry Klamer.

(skin boat), he said of his 1994 print *Taliilajukuluit*, "I would stare down into the water, in case I might see a Talilajuq."

A recurring subject in Andrew's prints is family. Of his 1994 print, *Our Loved One*, he said, "Out of love for my children, I wanted to show the *amautik* (mother's parka), where we all grew from. Beyond the family is a drying rack. There were a lot of them when Inuit still traded in sealskins. I remember the skins being rolled up in huge bundles." Childhood play is another favourite subject, often including a moral lesson. For example, about his 1992 print, *Playing Blindfold Games*, Andrew said, "You may never have thought of it this way before, but in this way [blindfolded] you learn respect for others who have handicaps."

By 2008 Andrew Qappik had produced 106 catalogued prints. Of those, 67 were made through the stencil process, a medium that permits the use of colour to maximum effect. However, his works also include 19 etchings, 9 stonecuts, 8 lithographs, 2 copper drypoints, and 1 linocut. In addition, Andrew produces many signed and editioned (but uncatalogued) "personal prints" identified by his personal chop that depicts a motionless Inuk poised over a seal hole. The latter prints are only available directly from the Uqqurmiut Centre for Arts and Crafts. The Winnipeg Art Gallery now owns virtually all of those as well. Unlike Cape Dorset artists, whose works are usually printed by others, Andrew produces most of his art himself, from drawings to numbered and signed prints. Only 46 years old in 2010, Andrew Qappik has a bright future; he is only now reaching his prime.

As a southern farm boy with no real knowledge of art, I compulsively collected all of Andrew's prints because I was intrigued watching the kid grow into a man and the eight-year-old caricaturist mature into a fine artist. Unfortunately, there is little interest in Inuit art in the American South so, when his productivity outgrew my "Andrew Room" in North Carolina, I wanted to return the retrospective collection to its national origin, Canada. Having known Darlene Wight through professional conferences and having admired her dedication to Inuit art and her publications on the subject, I am honoured to have the Winnipeg Art Gallery accept my collection of prints by Andrew Qappik.

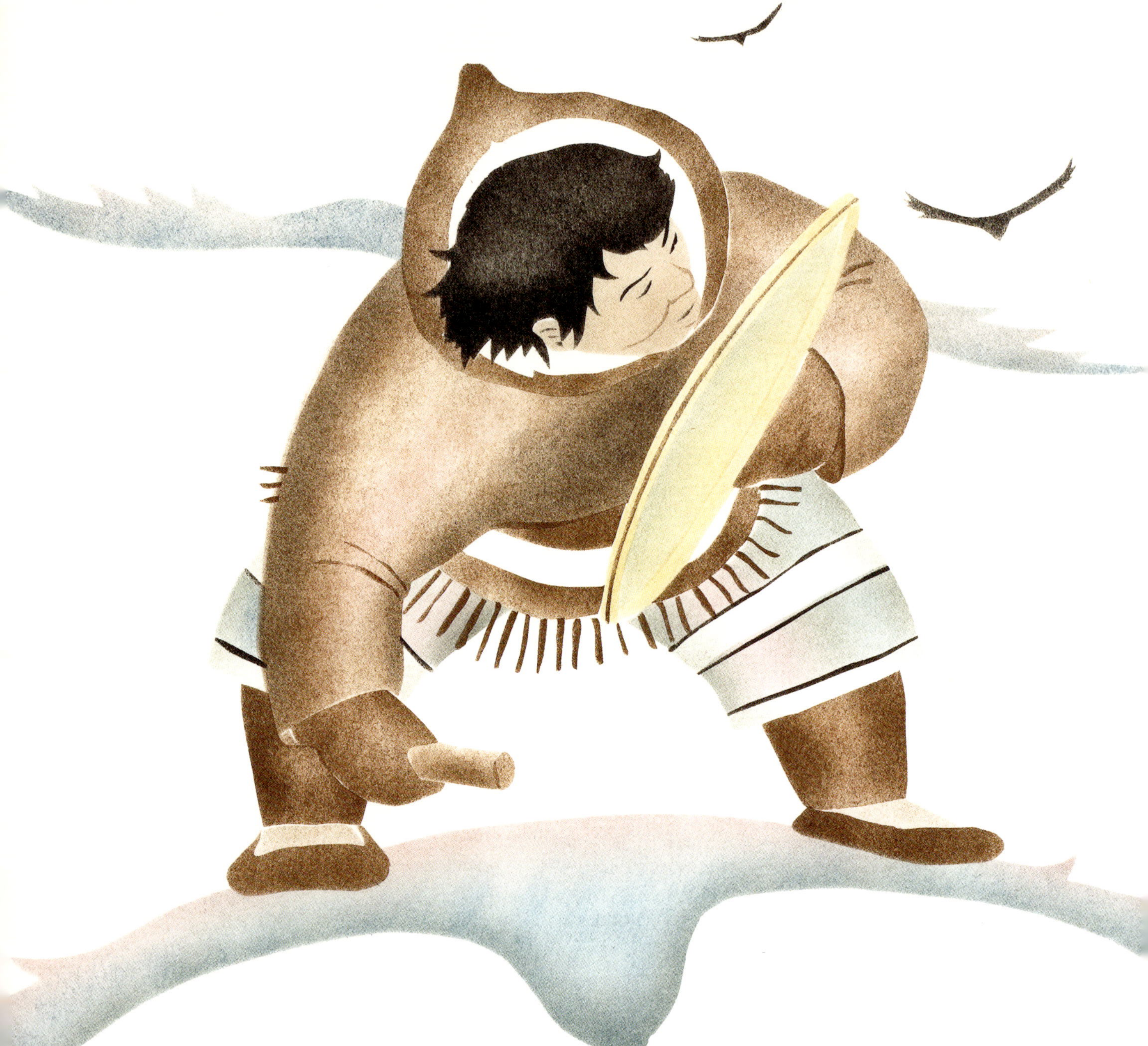

Andrew Qappik: Memory and Reality

Darlene Coward Wight, Curator of Inuit Art

Information is from a telephone interview conducted on March 16, 2010, unless referenced otherwise.

Andrew Qappik was born in 1964, in Nunataq, a family camp about 65 kilometres from the community of Pangnirtung.[1] The camp was that of his mother, Oleepa, and her family, including her parents, Eliyah Keenainak and his wife Martha.[2] Qappik's father, Mosesie Karpik, joined the camp when he married Oleepa. They had two children, Andrew and Mary.[3] The family moved off the land and into Pangnirtung when Qappik was still a baby.

Qappik first remembers making drawings when he was five or six years old. Solomon Karpik, his uncle, would ask the young Andrew to copy what Karpik had drawn. Qappik also made drawings of action figures from comic books that he, his family, and his friends collected. He remembers having stacks of comics that he often won through card games. He drew and painted with water-based paints in school art classes, and was encouraged by one teacher in particular whom he remembered as Miss Neil. He made portraits of other students as they worked on their lessons in class. When Qappik saw posters, he would copy them. He chuckled at a reminiscence of making a detailed drawing of a monkey from a poster. "Whenever I had paper and pencil, I would do sketches."

Qappik's involvement with the Pangnirtung Co-operative's print shop began in the mid-1970s.[4] His school conducted a work experience program, placing students in different workplaces in the community. Assigned to the print shop, Qappik remembers sweeping the floors and cleaning stencil brushes, but his involvement soon moved to a more creative level. John Houston was art advisor for the print program from 1975 to 1979, and he encouraged the creation of original drawings by having contests. Qappik decided to submit work for a contest in 1977 when he was 13 years old, and was awarded second prize by the printmakers. He remembers that his printed images for the 1977 collection were rejected by the Eskimo Arts Council as they "were too much like artists down south."[5] However, "the second year I did the same thing a little bit different, and they approved some of my work. They were sold out within a year." This was in 1978, when five of his drawings were translated into stencil prints for the annual print collection.

John Houston recently shared his memories of that period in Pangnirtung:

1 Qappik changed the spelling of his family name, Karpik, in 1994 to conform with modern orthography. **2** Martha died when Qappik was very young and he does not remember any other names. **3** Mary Etouangat is currently a teacher in Pangnirtung. **4** In 1969 printmaking was introduced in Pangnirtung as a project sponsored by the Government of the Northwest Territories. It was initiated under the supervision of Gary Magee, who encouraged the creation of drawings. The print program was taken over by the Pangnirtung Eskimo Co-operative (now the Pangnirtung Inuit Co-op Ltd.), which was incorporated in 1968. The first annual collection of prints was published by the Co-op in 1973. **5** The Canadian Eskimo Arts Council was established by the Department of Northern Affairs in 1961 and was intended to function as a professional arts advisory group for Inuit artists. It juried print collections and provided its embossed stamp of approval for all approved prints until it was disbanded in 1989. For further information, see Sue Gustavison, *Arctic Expressions: Inuit Art and the Canadian Eskimo Arts Council 1961–1989*, Kleinberg: McMichael Canadian Art Collection, 1994.

Qeelaujakluk (He plays the drum) (detail), 1997

We did hold drawing contests around that time, always searching for master drawings, and also searching for undiscovered talent. That was the most interesting thing about the period, to my mind—the rigorous experimentation, the multitude of proofs, the colour mixing—along with the drawing contests. We were all learning and growing together, and each day brought us new revelations.[6]

Houston remembers the young Qappik's intense interest at that time:

His passion was evident right at the beginning. Andrew came and hung out around the print shop, watched what everyone was doing, and after some time told us that he wanted to be a printmaker like his uncle Solomon. We told him that sounded like a good ambition for the future, if he still wanted to try it after completing his high school. Well, he didn't see why he should waste all that time in school when he already knew what he wanted to do with his life. There didn't seem to be anything we could say to change his mind, so we told him we'd take him on if his parents agreed. I figured that'd be the end of it, but shortly after that, there was Andrew, with his parents in tow. We all listened to his passion, his dream, to his reasoning why we should let him apprentice to become a printmaker, starting right away. And it must be true, what they say about the power of daring to dream, because shortly after that the Pangnirtung print shop had a new apprentice—our youngest ever. And look at his work today![7]

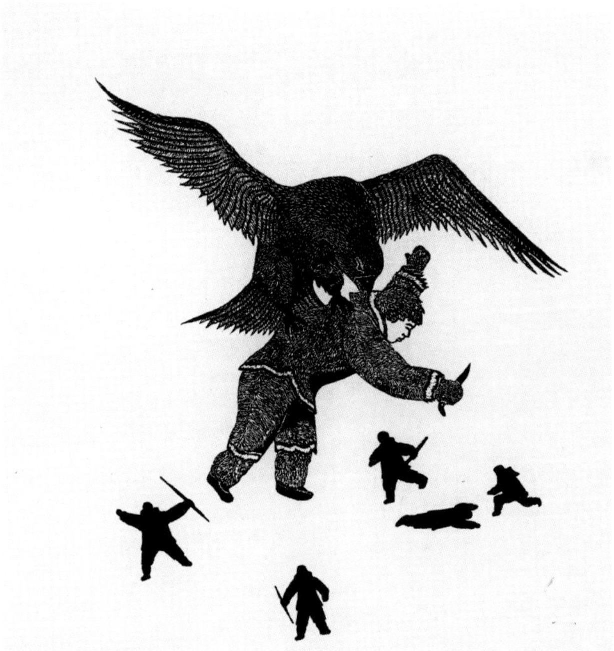
The Hunter Bird, 1983

Qappik first printed two of his own drawings, *The Great Hunter* and *The Hunter Bird*, for the 1983 collection using the stonecut technique, learned from his uncle:

I was first taught as a stonecut printmaker by my uncle Solomon Karpik. He said when I first started that I would be a stonecut printmaker. That would be my trade. He taught me how to carve the stone, how to scratch the surface, how to smooth and grind the stone before working on it; how to use speed-ball rollers, mix colour, and use two or three different colours on the same roll. Those kinds of techniques he used, he taught me.

In 1983 the Pangnirtung Eskimo Co-operative hired Stephen Osler, a printmaker from Nova Scotia, to act as its art advisor. He gave instruction in etching and aquatint, and in 1985 Qappik used these techniques in the piece *Net Fishing* (p.22), as well as in *Char Fishing* (p.23) the following year. In October 1986 a lithography workshop was conducted by visiting artist Don Holman, from the University of Toronto. In March 1987 master printer Pitseolak Niviaqsi travelled from

Cape Dorset to give further training in lithography. Qappik produced his first lithograph in 1987.

Under the auspices of the Pangnirtung Eskimo Co-operative, annual print collections were produced from 1975–1980 and 1983–1988. However, the print shop was forced to close in 1988 as the Co-op and territorial government could no longer support it financially. Refusing to accept the end of their art-making, the artists and printmakers began meeting to determine a course of action. In April 1988 the Uqqurmiut Inuit Artists Association was incorporated as a fully Inuit-owned and Inuit-run organization with a clear mission:

> *To serve Pangnirtung artists and the community of Pangnirtung, to keep all of their arts and culture alive, and to ensure their full participation and control by creating employment and training opportunities for artists, providing a central place for the creation and marketing of art, contributing to local tourism, and providing an art archive to preserve the art for future generations.*[8]

The artists began raising funds to build a new arts centre—the first to be owned and operated by an independent group of Inuit artists. The Uqqurmiut Centre for Arts & Crafts became a reality over the winter of 1990–1991 and had its official opening on May 31, 1991.

The Uqqurmiut Centre included new space for the Pangnirtung Tapestry Studio. Woven wool tapestries had been created in Pangnirtung since 1970, with the weavers using drawing designs by graphic artists for their cartoons. Qappik's drawings were first used to

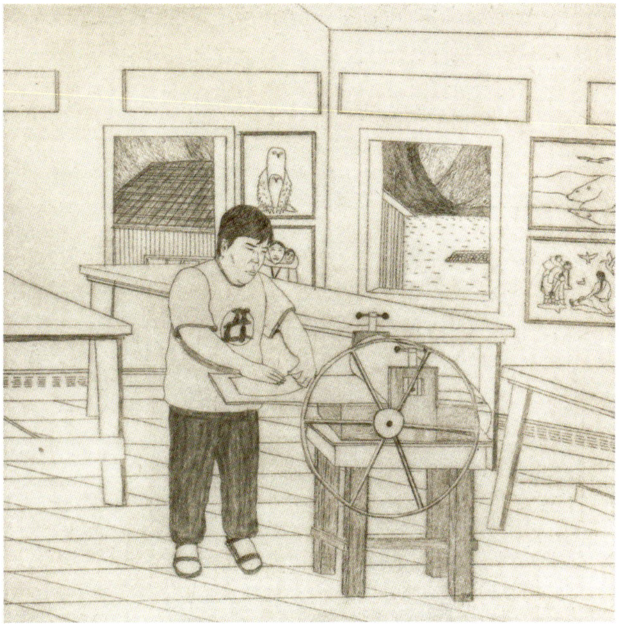

Andrew Qappik (Self-Portrait in Printshop), 2003

create tapestries in 1992 when he collaborated with other artists and weavers on *Our Ancestors Land is Our Land Now*, a large government commission for the Unikkaarvik Visitor Centre in Iqaluit. In 1998 *My Puppies* was based on a drawing by Qappik and woven by Olassie Akulukjuuk.[9] That same year another of Qappik's drawings was used for the tapestry *Checking the Seal Hole*, created by Anna Etoangat. The following year he designed the tapestry *Fear of Killer Whale*, which was later used on the cover of the 2002–2003 NorthwesTel Directory.

With new space created in the Uqqurmiut Centre for a tapestry studio, the old weaving shop was renovated in 1992 for use as a new Print Shop, and the first print collection in four years was published, now called *The Pangnirtung Community Print Collection*. Printers were

6 Email message from John Houston, March 21, 2010. 7 Ibid. 8 Uqqurmiut Centre website 9 *My Puppies* was included in the major exhibition *Nuvisavik: the place where we weave*, organized and toured by the Canadian Museum of Civilization in 2002.

no longer paid a salary and remuneration was dependent upon sale of their works. Prints were embossed with a new stamp: the Inuktitut syllabics for the word *piujiuq* (very good), in addition to the traditional *qatanquaq* chop (entrance to the iglu). Don Holman returned to give further instruction to the printmakers, and worked with Qappik on the innovative lithograph *Hunter's Dream* (p.29). The use of this lithographic technique expresses the realistic details of Qappik's original drawing, including caribou footprints in the snow.

Qappik made his first stencils in 1993. Veils of transparent colour give a new delicacy to his gentle subjects placed within full landcapes. In *Favourite Place To Be* (p.30), the paper is completely covered with nuanced colours that give different viewpoints, above and below the ice. By this time, the use of multiple perspectives had become a trademark of Qappik's style.

Disaster struck the Print Shop in 1994, just as the artists were rebounding from their previous years without a place to work. Fire destroyed the Print Shop on March 29, including the etching and litho presses. Incredibly, the artists created new drawings, and stencils were used to print them for a collection that same year. Qappik created five stencil prints for that collection.

With typical determination, the printmakers and community leaders worked together to construct a new Print Shop as part of the Uqqurmiut Centre. It is a spacious 325 square metre building with an archival area used to house the Centre's 10,000 drawings and prints. The printmakers were able to use the new building to create a 1996 print collection. In June of 1996 master printer Paul Machnik of Montreal came to Pangnirtung for three weeks to help set up the new Print Shop for etching, working with the local artists to prepare plates for printing. A new etching press was used to create 15 of the 24 prints published that year.

For Qappik, however, stencil became his main mode of expression for the next few years. He created exquisite wildlife studies, such as *Early Summer Loons* (p.35), *Underwater Char* (p.36), and *Shore Birds* (p.37), in which translucent veils of colour express watery reflections, refraction of light under water, and shimmering sand. In 2003 he resumed the use of etching and aquatint to interpret some of his most intimate family scenes: *Long Journey Ahead* (p.39), *String Games* (p.43), and *My Daughter Ceporah and Buffy* (p.42). The latter print is a portrait, made from the memory of a family photograph. In 2008 etching

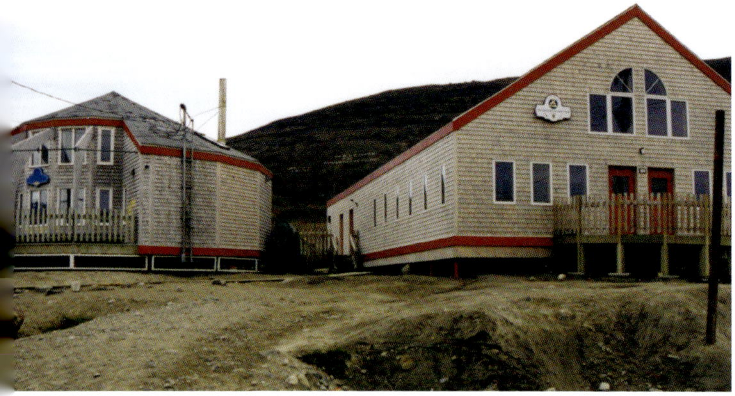

Uqqurmiut Centre for Arts & Crafts. Photo by H.G. Jones.

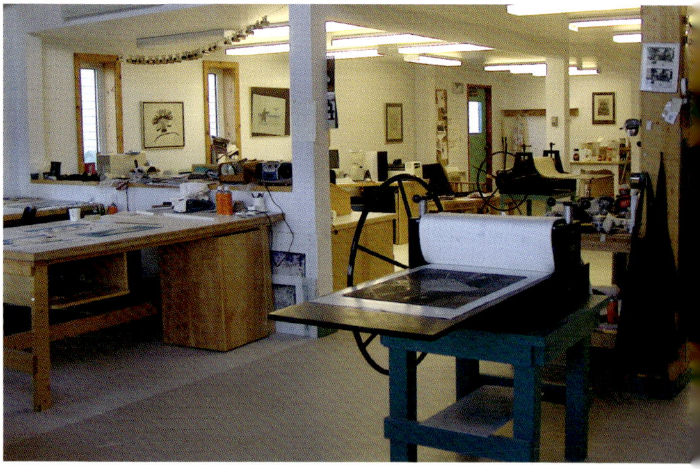

Uqqurmiut Print Shop. Photo by Kyra V. Fisher.

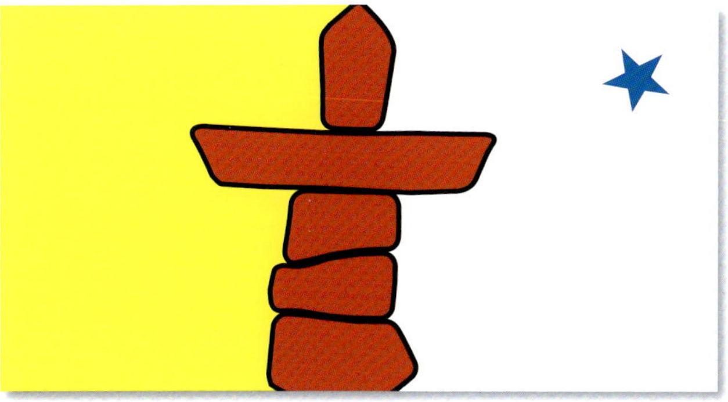

expressed a more ominous scene in *Whales Ahead* (p.44), as tense hunters row toward their distant quarry in a small *umiak* (skin boat). The sky and water are dark, giving a sense of danger to the hunters' pursuit.

Qappik had also used etching in 1988 for a series of three portraits of elders, created from photographs. One of these, *Pauloosie Karpik* (p.27), depicted his grandfather in reverential detail.[10] These portraits reveal the artist's respect for elder members of the community, a respect often evident in his comments as well. In Qappik's most recent prints, stencil continues to be used for delicate landscapes, such as his pure landscape *Panniqtuuq* (p.44), and his animal prints, such as *Arctic Wolfs* [sic] (p.38).

Wildlife holds a special place in Qappik's work. The appeal of this subject matter in his works lies in the fact that the images are not purely realistic translations of external appearances. Qappik has explained that, "I try to put the character in—if the animals are upbeat or playful—so it's not just an animal." In *Arctic Wolfs* (p.38), the stealth, cunning, and aggression of the animals is expressed as they slink low to the ground, straight toward the viewer. They are following the snowy footprints of their animal quarry, much as their human hunter counterparts would do. The dark eyes, nose, and ears of each animal are visible first as the forms emerge, in subtle shades of white, from a snowy white background.

In the early 1990s, Qappik began to receive a number of commissions and honours. He was hired by the Baffin Divisional Board of Education to create illustrations for a series of school textbooks in Inuktitut. The Canadian Coast Guard created a poster promoting boat safety from one of his drawings. In 1995 his work was included in the exhibition *Keeping Our Stories Alive* at the Institute of American Indian Arts in Santa Fe, New Mexico.

Qappik's career reached a new high point with the ceremonies to mark the creation of the new territory of Nunavut held in Iqaluit on April 1, 1999. The new territorial flag and coat of arms based on his designs were first revealed to the public after a two-year selection process. In May 1997 a nation-wide contest

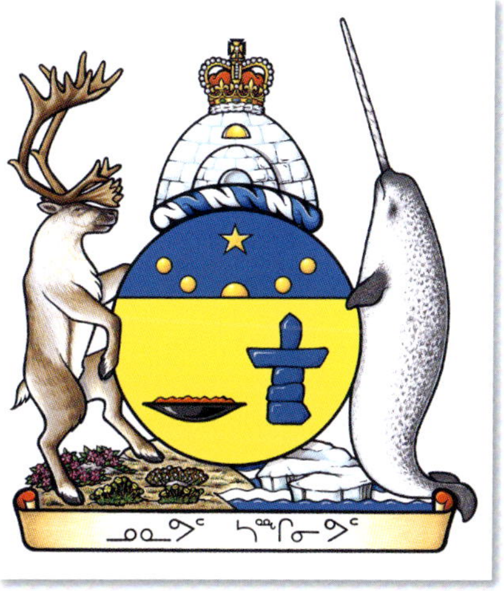

10 Pauloosie Karpik (1911–1988) was Qappik's paternal grandfather. Solomon Karpik and Imoona Karpik are Pauloosie's stepsons, as their mother married Pauloosie after the death of her first husband. See H.G. Jones, *Inuit Art Quarterly* 1991. Jones describes the circumstances under which Pauloosie's first drawings were created in the early 1960s. From 1976 to 1988, 17 prints were created from his drawings.

had begun with an invitation from the Nunavut Implementation Committee (NIC) to artists to submit designs for both the flag and the coat of arms. By February 1998 over 800 submissions had been received. They were reviewed in the spring of 1998 by a jury consisting of NIC Symbols Committee Chair Meeka Kilabuk; Nunavut Tunngavik Incorporated President Jose Kusugak; NIC Chairman John Amagoalik; and Canada's Chief Herald, Robert Watt; as well as the artists Kanaginak Pootoogook (Cape Dorset), Thomas Iksiraq (Baker Lake), and Nick Sikkuarq (Kugaaruk). Images created by Qappik were chosen as draft versions of the flag and the coat of arms, and then merged with the motifs of the other finalists.[11]

Qappik remembers the submission process with a degree of humour:

> *I first sketched those [designs] on my way back from the Great Northern Arts Festival in Inuvik. I made drawings at the Yellowknife Inn. On my way back I had to go through Iqaluit, and it was the last day to submit my artwork. I dropped them off where the commissioners were receiving submissions for the flag and coat of arms. On my way there, getting out of a car, my pants ripped. I was hurrying to submit my artwork. I felt sorry I had to submit my artwork with my pants ripped.*

After being informed of his selection to work on the final designs (and sworn to secrecy), Qappik travelled to Ottawa twice to work with Cathy Bursey-Sabourin, principal artist for the Canadian Heraldic Authority, to finalize details of the designs, which were approved by Queen Elizabeth II in October 1998. Qappik describes some of this process:

> *They told me I had to go and work in Ottawa, to do more work on what I had submitted to them. I had two walls covered with the same flag design, but shown in different ways. One was chosen. For the coat of arms, they asked me if I could add a little bit of artwork into my art. I added an iglu on the top, and a* qulliq, *a seal-oil lamp. For the seasons, the sun dipping in, that was someone else's design that I put together into my artwork. I only had a week or two to finish the work for the flag and the coat of arms.*

Another honour came to Qappik in February 2000 when a new logo for the Government of Nunavut, based on his drawing of a polar bear, was unveiled in Rankin Inlet by then Premier Paul Okalik. The logo has become widely visible as it is used on government signs, forms, letterhead, and other visual media. During the unveiling, Okalik said the logo "embodies

11 *Inuit Art Quarterly*, Fall 1999. **12** Nunatsiaq News, February 25, 2000 **13** Ibid. **14** Fisher, *Inuit Art Quarterly*, 2010.

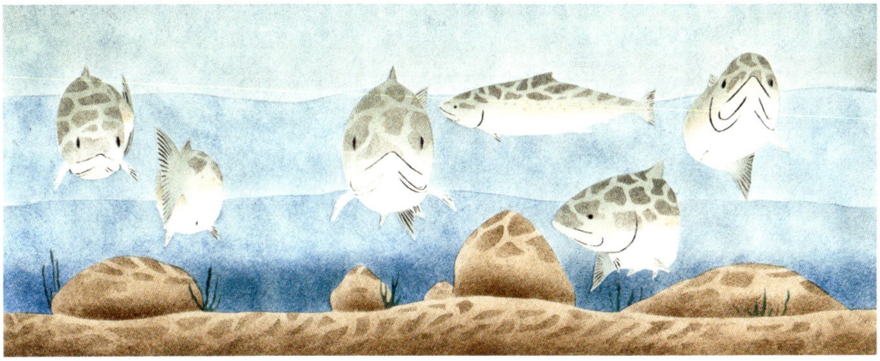

Underwater Char, 1998

that represents 55,000 Inuit across Canada). This lively and colourful tapestry greeted visitors to the Richmond Oval, the speed skating venue, and will remain at this site. It includes images by Dinah Anderson of Labrador; Sammy J. Kudluk of Kuujjuaq, Nunavik; Mabel Nigiyok and Louie Nigiyok of Holman.

While printmaking at the Uqqurmiut Centre was suspended for 2009, three workshops were organized in the fall by General Manager Kyra Fisher to give artists and printmakers training in new materials and techniques, and to encourage participation by younger artists.[14] In November Danny Osborne, a British artist now living in Iqaluit, gave instruction in oil painting, a technique

the qualities of strength and determination evident in the people of Nunavut.... The polar bear is moving forward to a more prosperous Nunavut, while looking back into the past, acknowledging the traditions of the Inuit way of life and teachings of the elders."[12] Qappik has added that he wanted to convey the strength of the polar bear as it looked back to Inuit history, but moved forward into the future.[13]

Qappik's own future is promising. In 2003 he received the Queen Elizabeth Jubilee Medal and was honoured with membership in the Royal Canadian Academy of Arts. In 2005 the National Film Board produced a short film, *I Can Make Art Like Andrew Qappik*, which documented Qappik's instructions to a group of school-age children on the creation process for stencil prints. In 2006 Qappik conducted a printmaking workshop in Iqaluit during the Arctic Winter Games.

2009 was a busy year for Qappik. On January 9 the Royal Canadian Mint issued a $100, 14-karat gold coin commemorating the 10th anniversary of the creation of Nunavut, based on a design by Qappik. He was the lead designer of a major tapestry, *Achieving a Dream*, commissioned by the Vancouver Organizing Committee for the 2010 Olympic Winter Games through the Inuit Tapiriit Kanatami (an organization

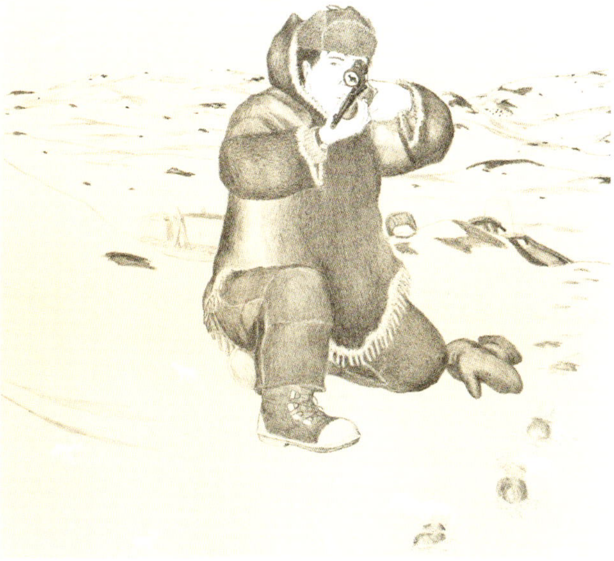

Hunter's Dream, 1992

that was new to the artists and printmakers. Qappik participated in the workshop and created *People of Pangnirtung* (p.45) at that time. This first significant painting by the artist has been acquired by the Winnipeg Art Gallery and is included in this exhibition.

The detailed style of this painting is consistent with that of Qappik's prints and drawings. He makes sophisticated use of shading, perspective, and foreshortening to give realistic volume and depth to his subjects and to their fully realized settings. However, the medium of oil gives him new scope for colour-based effects. Clothing of seal fur (grey) and dehaired sealskin (brown) is shown in lingering detail. Delicate layers and gradations of colour reveal transparent reflections in the water. The mountainous landscape is a vast, three-dimensional space that invites the eye into its depths.

Andrew Qappik marks the third generation of Inuit who have been creating art for world markets since the early 1950s. Born on the land in a traditional camp, he has spent all but a couple of years living in the community of Pangnirtung. He grew up listening to stories of earlier times told to him by elders, particularly his grandfathers Pauloosie Karpik and Eliyah Keenainak, and his uncle Solomon Karpik. The vivid memories of these respected elders have been his greatest source of subject matter. His comments often reveal the nostalgia, even escapism, of his thinking about the past:

> *When I hear the elders tell the stories of whaling in the past, it makes me dream. How was it to prosper without any machinery, not knowing where the whale will surface, using your instinct to direct the* umiaq*? I wish I was there, when there were no worries about anything, but to survive!* [15]

While growing up in the community, Qappik was exposed to imported visual stimuli, such as comic books, posters, books, and television. His visual acuity allowed him to absorb Western conventions of image-making. By drawing the action figures from comics, he learned how to animate his drawn subjects. He delights in using his facility with perspective by showing his subjects from various points of view, as exemplified by the 1998 print *Underwater Char* (p.36). Fish are foreshortened at different angles and rounded into three-dimensional forms through shading. While fully adept at using three-point perspective, he sometimes uses multiple perspectives to show different parts of a scene: "I like to show things in a different perspective. Looking down or looking up, like a person looking through a seal breathing hole and seeing a seal under the ice. Showing the seal, but also a dog above, interested in what his master is doing."[16]

There is a strong storytelling impetus in Qappik's work that is facilitated by his multiple perspectives and his use of very fine detailing.[17] The quarry in *Hunter's Dream* (p.29) is revealed by the tiny reflection of a caribou in the scope of the gun and the footprints in the snow. At first glance, the etching *Approaching the Caribou Pass* (p.25) could be an animal study, but closer examination reveals hunters arriving in boats in the distant background and a plot develops. The viewer realizes why the caribou are warily sniffing the air.

The use of fine and often unexpected details appears in another etching, *With Open Mind* (p.28). The viewer realizes that one walrus has the tail of a whale and the shadow under the front walrus is actually a miniature team of dogs pulling a sled. The subject of the stencil print *Qeelaujakluk* (p.33) is not only a drum dancer but an expression of the artist's wish to revive the skills of the drum dance. He shows the dancer's shadow in the form of a bird which grows

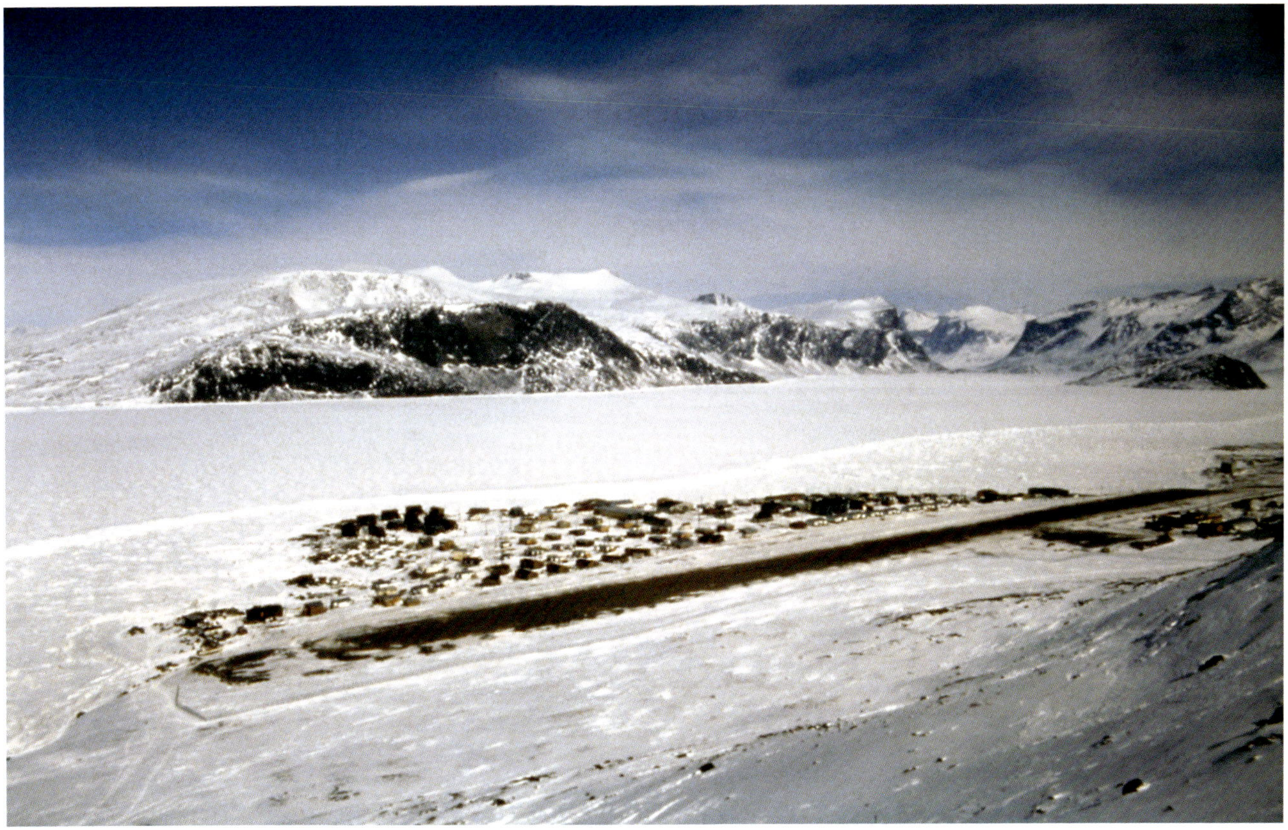

Pangnirtung, 1989. Photo by Carey Archibald.

ever larger as it moves into the present (see caption). Small details draw the viewer into the works and into the story being told.

When asked how he gets his ideas for his art, Qappik states, "Everything is based on my culture." He is profoundly religious, and does much work for his church.[18] He and his wife Annie maintain a shelter in their home for women who are being mistreated. Respect for his ancestors, their history, his culture, and a desire to show these to the world take on a similar passion. In his artwork, this respect for his people, his past, and his place in the fiords of east Baffin Island, is interpreted through a realistic style of European drawing conventions and printing techniques. Recent experimentation in the medium of oil paint continues the merging of the past and the present, as he and his generation come to terms with their cultural identity in a rapidly changing environment.

15 Artist in Pangnirtung Community Print Collection, 1992, no.13. **16** Telephone interview with Wight, March 16, 2010. **17** Qappik heard many stories from his father, Mosesie Karpik, as well as his grandparents and other members of his family. **18** Qappik's maternal grandfather, Eliyak Keenainak, was a Canon in the Anglican Church.

Notes to the catalogue

All prints are in the collection of the Winnipeg Art Gallery and are a gift of Dr. H.G. Jones. The painting, *People of Pangnirtung*, was purchased by the Gallery with funds from the RH Foundation.

Dates followed by numbers refer to annual print catalogues published as follows: Government of the Northwest Territories, 1973; Pangnirtung Eskimo Co-operative, 1975–1988; Uqqurmiut Inuit Artists Association, 1992–2008.

"Uncatalogued" indicates an unpublished print created independently by the artist.

Prints are in chronological order. Dimensions of all works are height x width (cm).

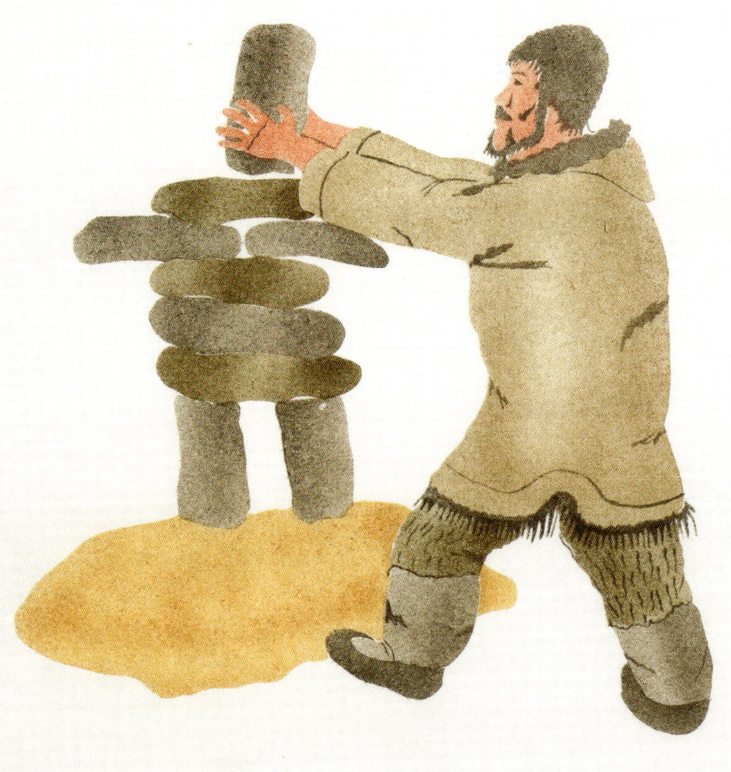

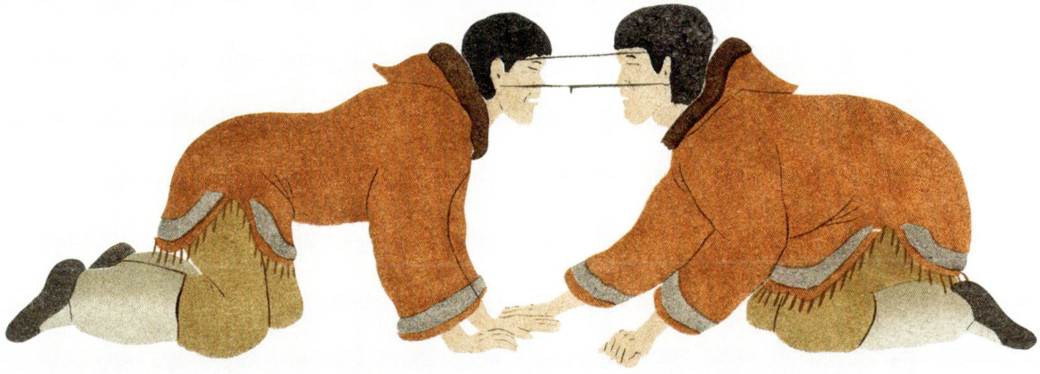

Making Inukshuk, 1978–#8
Printmaker: Mosesie Nuvaqirq, b. 1945
Stencil 38/50
41.0 x 38.4
2006-239

Ear-Pulling Contest, 1979–#13
Printmaker: Josea Maniapik, b. 1941
Stencil 39/50
31.5 x 55.0
2006-246

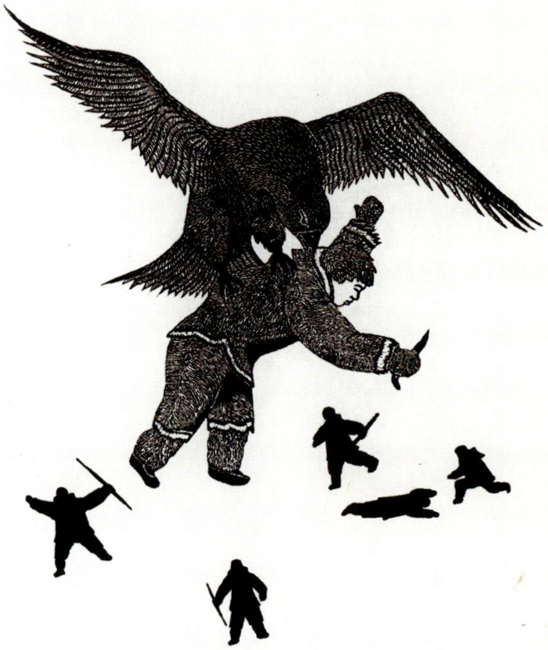

The Hunter Bird, 1983–#15
Stonecut 38/50
56.3 x 49.5
2006-250

Net Fishing, 1985–#19
Etching 12/50
41.5 x 92.0
2006-258

Char Fishing, 1986–#13
Etching; aquatint 47/50
56.5 x 37.5
2006-260

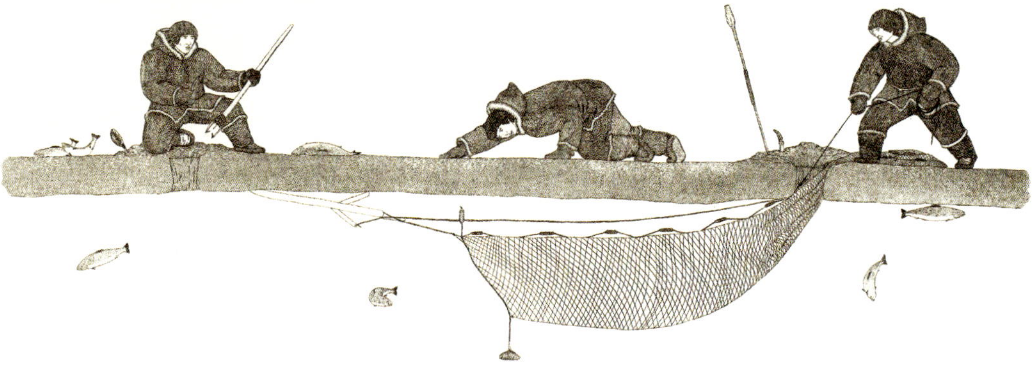

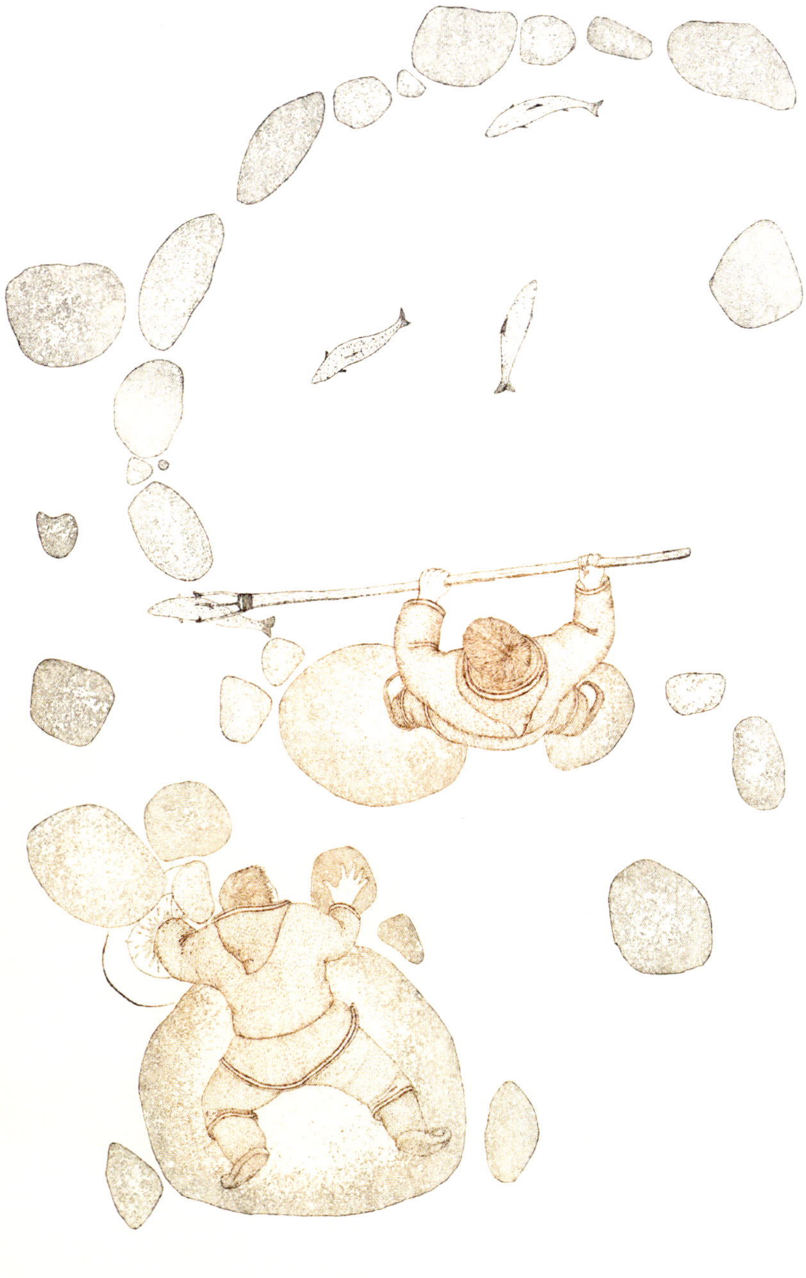

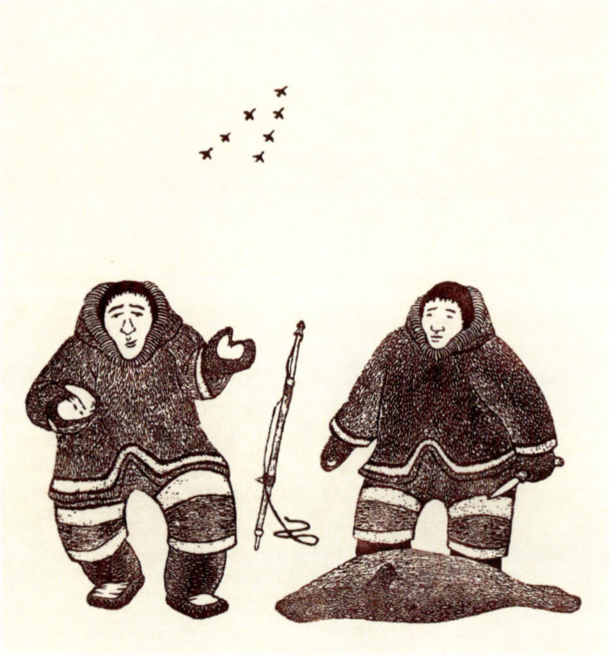

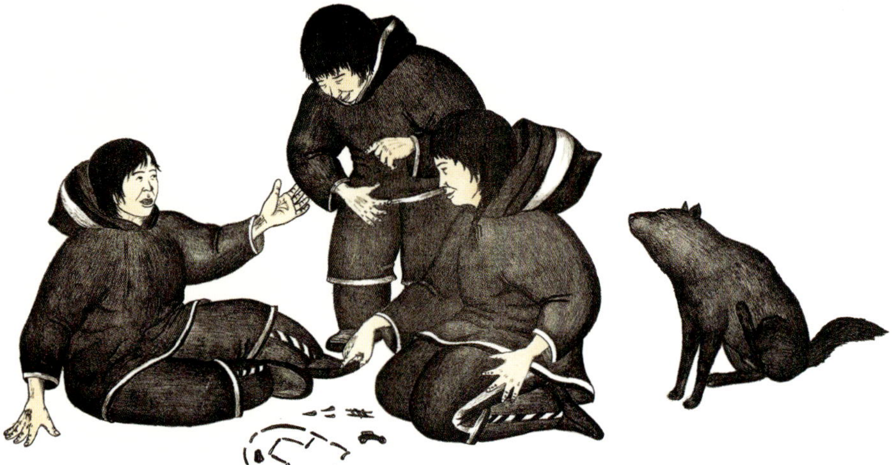

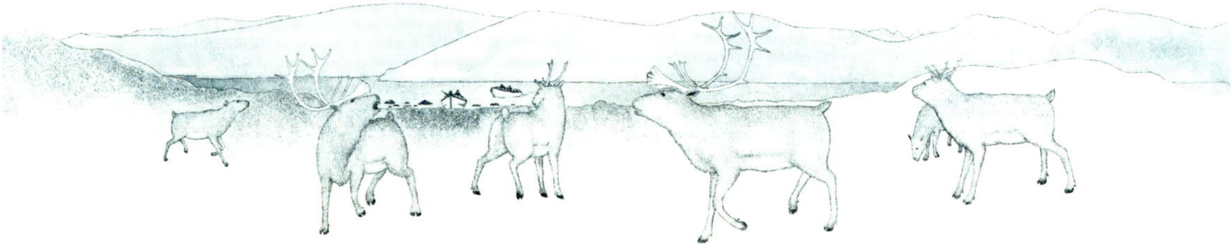

Protest, 1986–#14
Stonecut 42/50
36.8 x 32.5
2006-261

Wishing Bone Game, 1987–#6
Lithograph 44/50
44.7 x 68.8
2006-262

Approaching the Caribou Pass, 1987–#7
Etching; aquatint 44/50
46.0 x 94.0
2006-263

In Searching for Food, *I started out with wolves, to see if I could make them. The idea for the drawing came quickly, and I just drew it, thinking of them as hungry wolves, searching for food.*

—Artist in *Pangnirtung 1987 Prints*, 1987

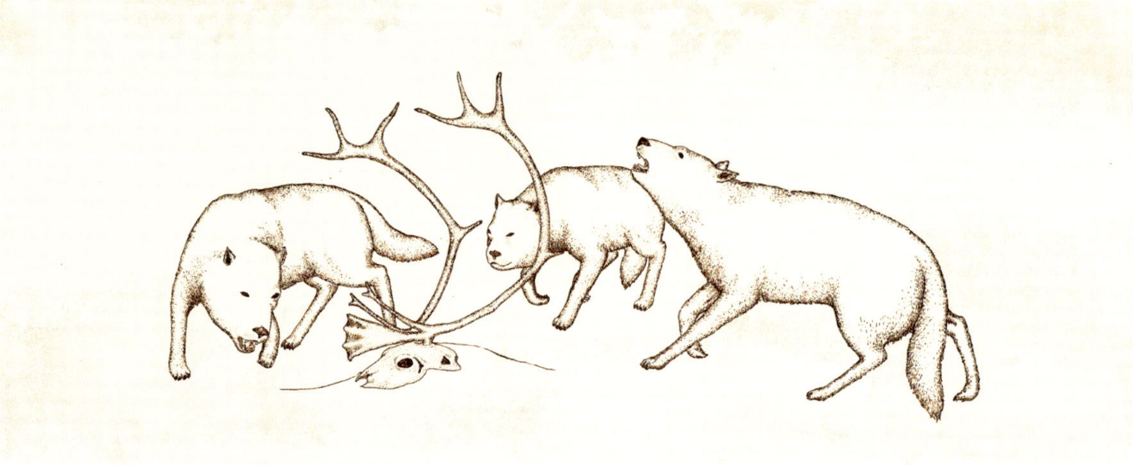

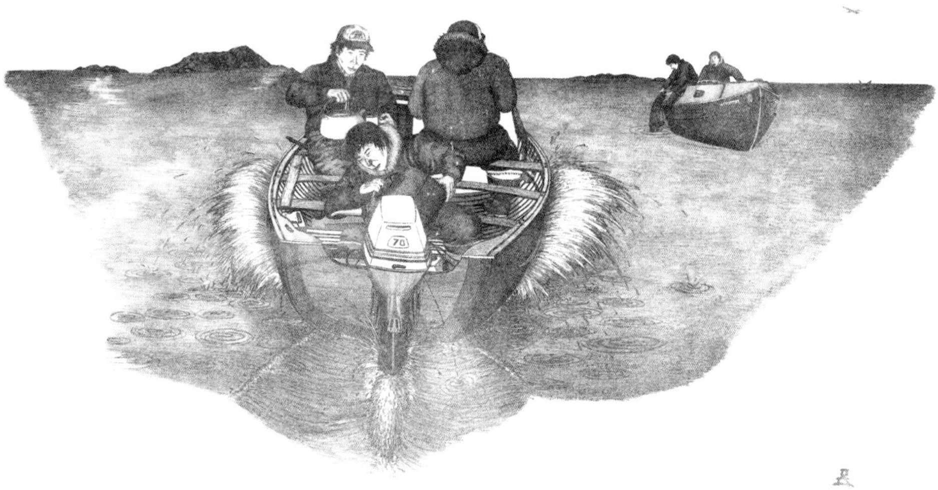

Searching for Food, 1987–#8
Etching; aquatint 18/35
35.4 x 56.3
2006-264

Summer Outfitting, 1988–#4
Lithograph 8/15
53.5 x 84.0
2006-266

Pauloosie Karpik, 1988–#7
Lithograph 8/35
43.3 x 35.3
2006-269

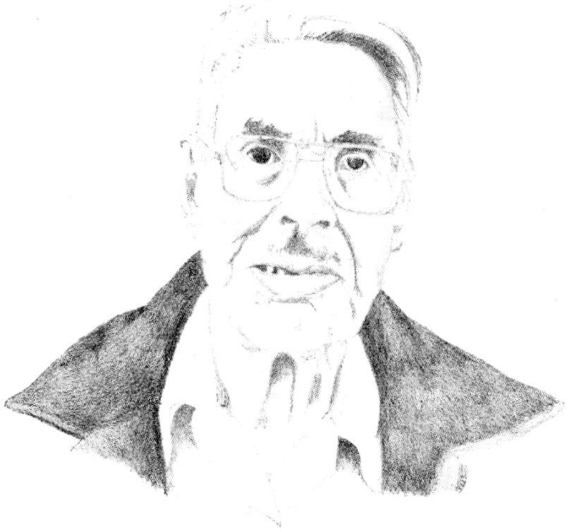

Our heritage includes shamanism. A shaman would have a champion animal which he or she could become. This animal would be dominant over others, like the walrus is feared by the killer whale. Today the transformation occurs in humans with an open mind. You can know so much more of others' ways of life today, and learning this, something you never knew before, this knowledge becomes part of you.

—Artist in *Pangnirtung Community Print Collection*, 1992

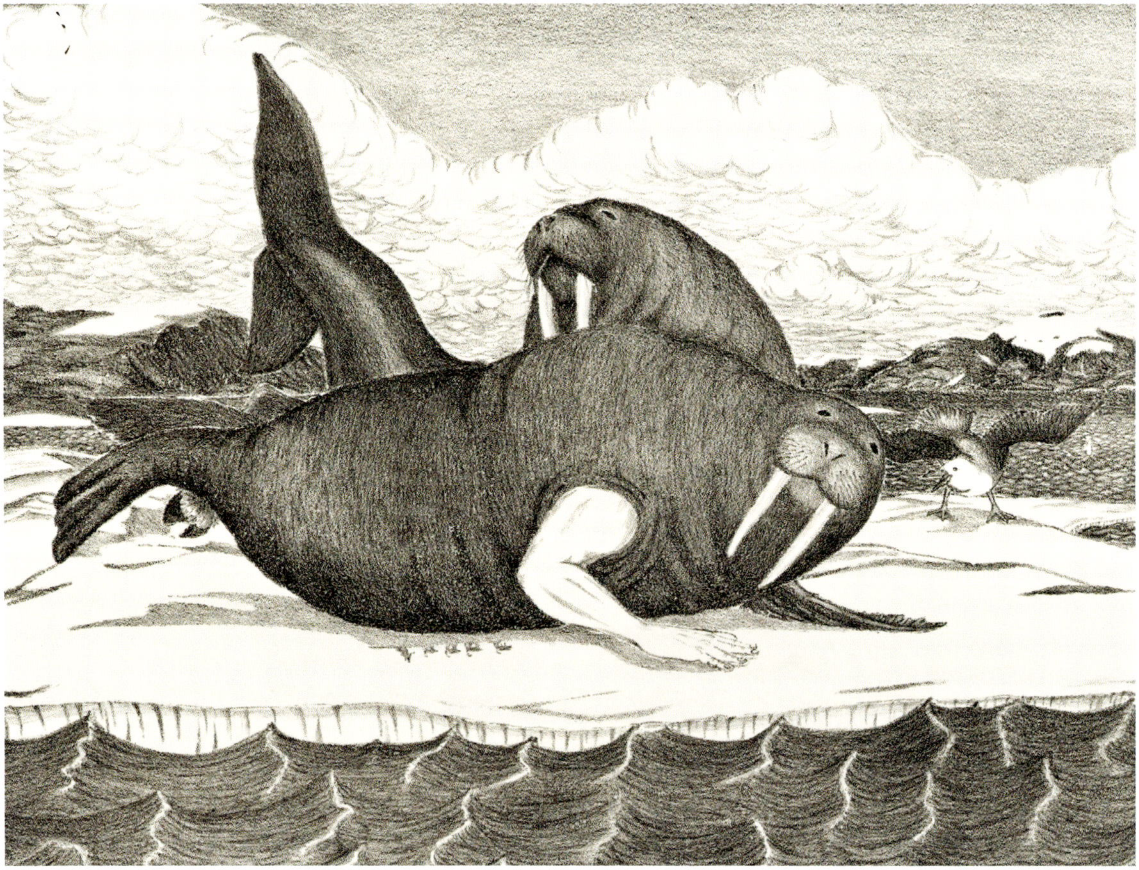

With Open Mind, 1992–#12
Lithograph 19/45
39.2 x 48.7
2006-271

Hunter's Dream, 1992–#16
Printmakers: Don Holman, Andrew Qappik
Lithograph 30/50
45.7 x 38.0
2006-275

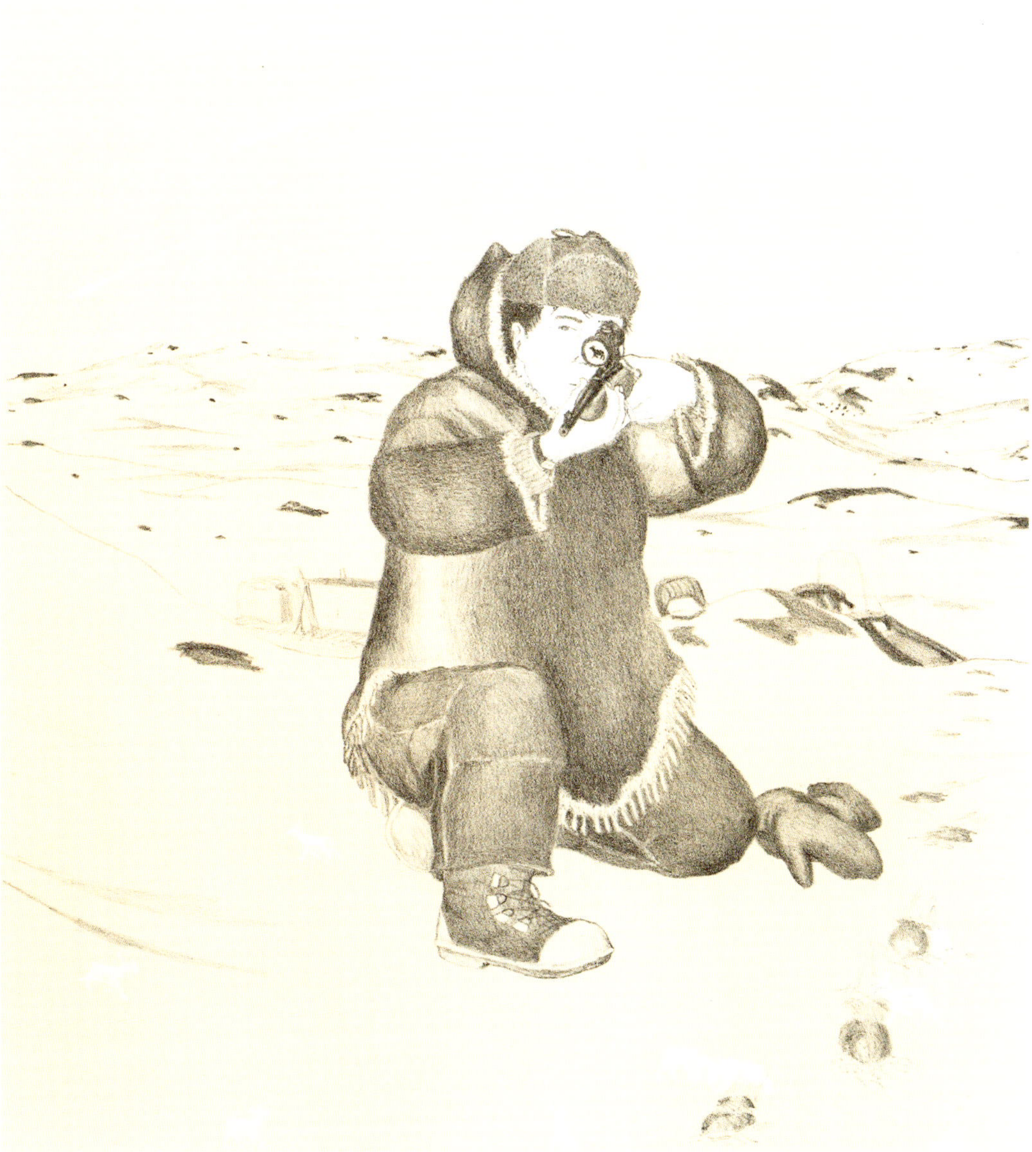

As I aim at the caribou through the scope of the gun, I think of how my ancestors survived with a bow and arrow, harvesting the caribou to support our families through the generations.

—Artist in *Pangnirtung Community Print Collection*, 1992

Waiting for a fish through a hole in the ice takes a little patience. In the winter time, people would try to spear a fish, using a kakivak and a bait.

—Artist in *Pangnirtung Community Print Collection*, 1993

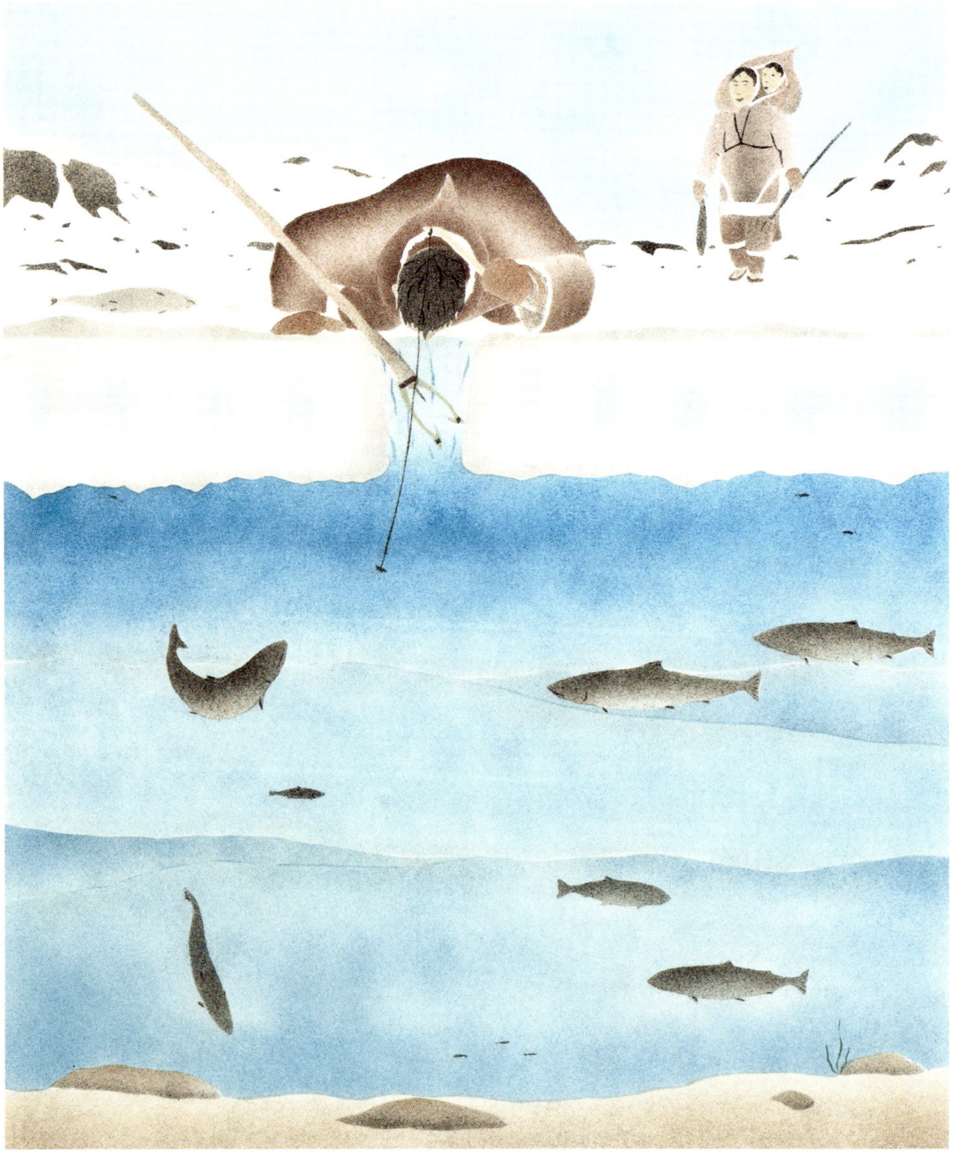

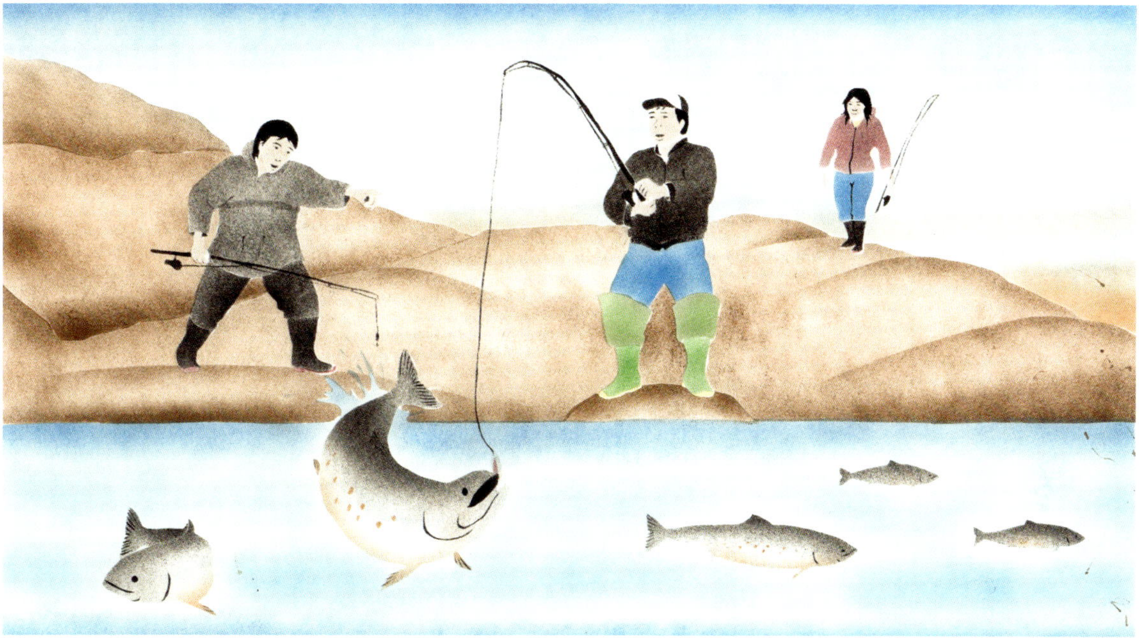

Favourite Place to Be, 1993–#16
Stencil 34/50
50.7 x 43.7
2006-279

Fishing at Ingalik, 1996–#15
Stencil 20/50
39.2 x 64.5
2006-292

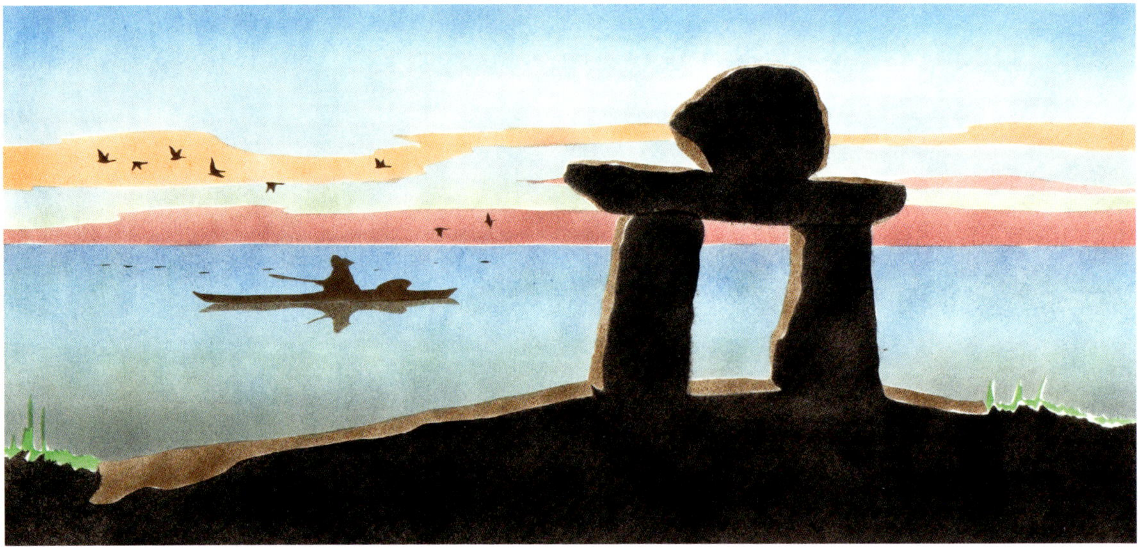

Specified Route, 1996 (uncatalogued)
Stencil 9/50
27.8 x 54.5
2006–356

Qeelaujakluk (He plays the drum), 1997–#8
Stencil 22/40
40.5 x 53.7
2006-296

I'd like to have drum dancing come alive, to have drummers start drumming again. So I tried to portray that in this print. The drummer has a shadow like a bird. It's like a drummer is coming back again after a long journey. The bird is in the distance small, getting larger and larger until you see him in the front. I wanted to put my thoughts into my artwork.

I do volunteer work in youth care at our church and we were invited to go to Ireland a couple of years ago. One of our ladies brought a drum. We sang some hymns using the drum at their Parliament. People were very amazed.

(Telephone interview with artist, March 16, 2010)

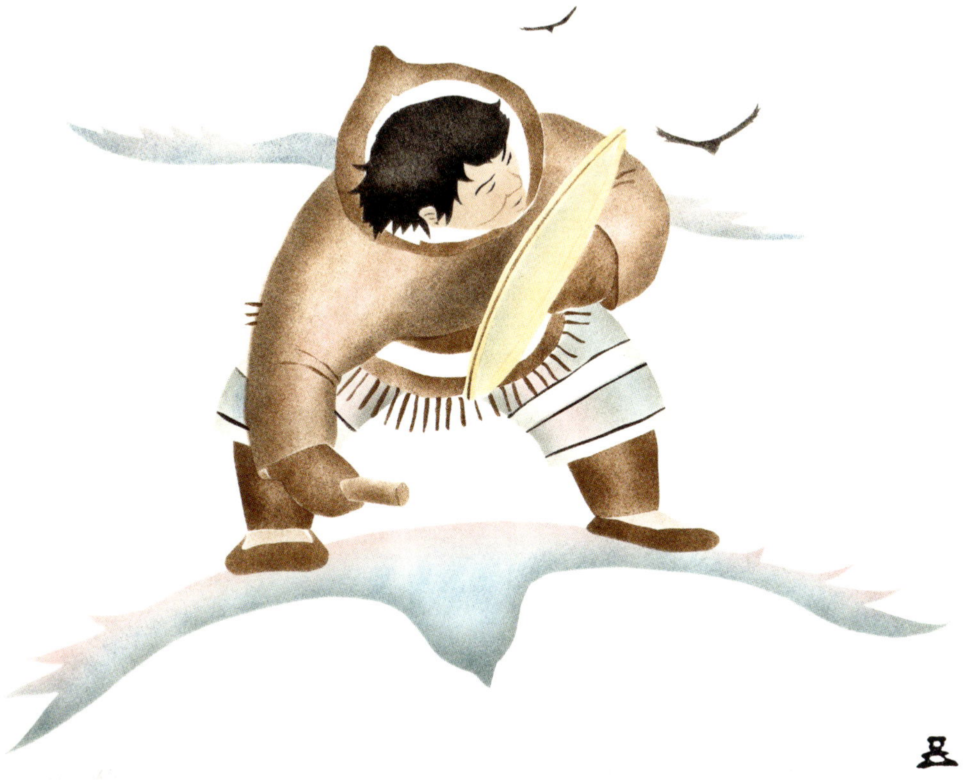

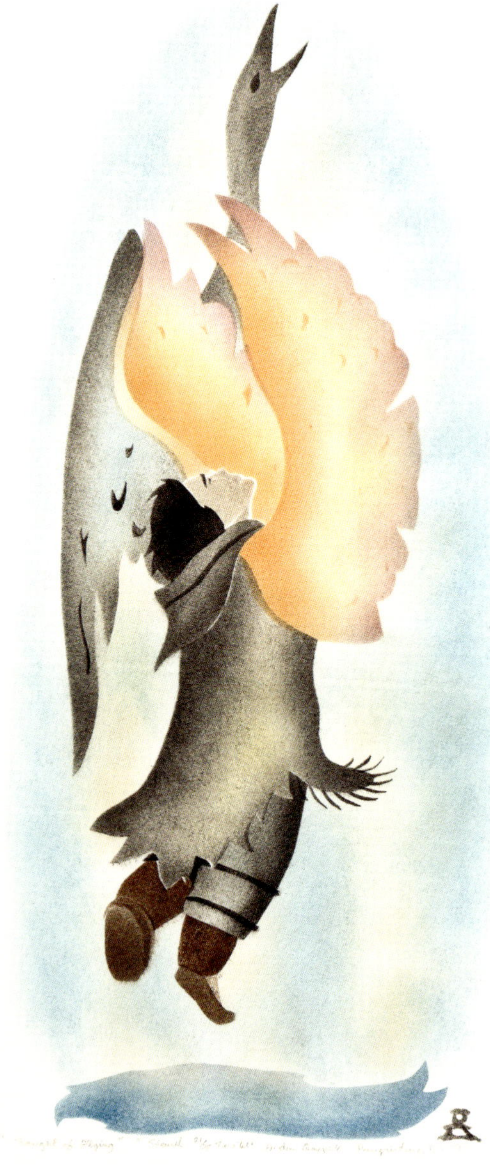

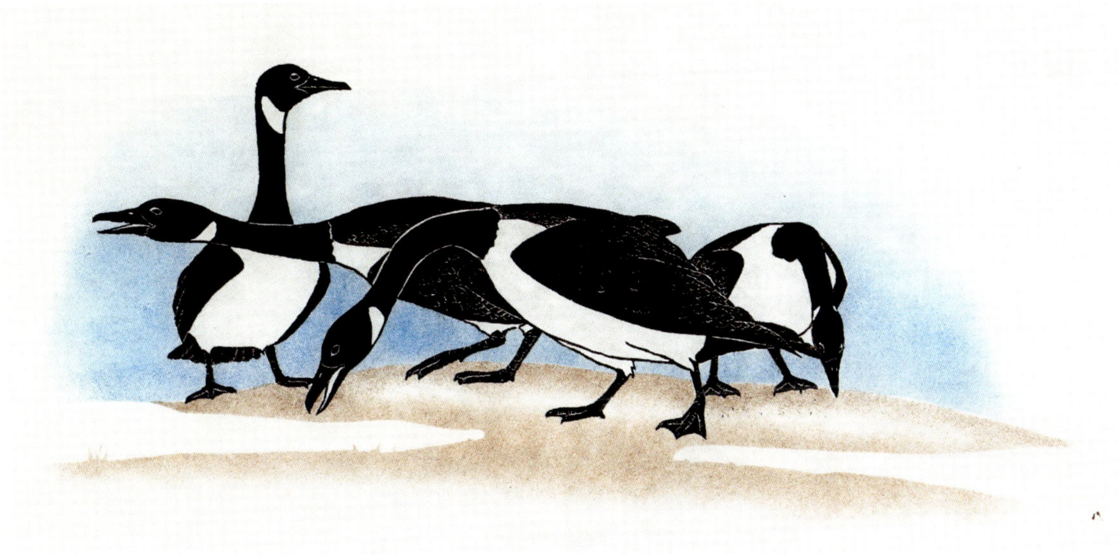

Thought of Flying, 1997 (uncatalogued)
Stencil 21/75
56.5 x 25.0
2006-360

Early Summer Loons, 1998–#6
Stencil 20/50
32.7 x 64.0
2006-300

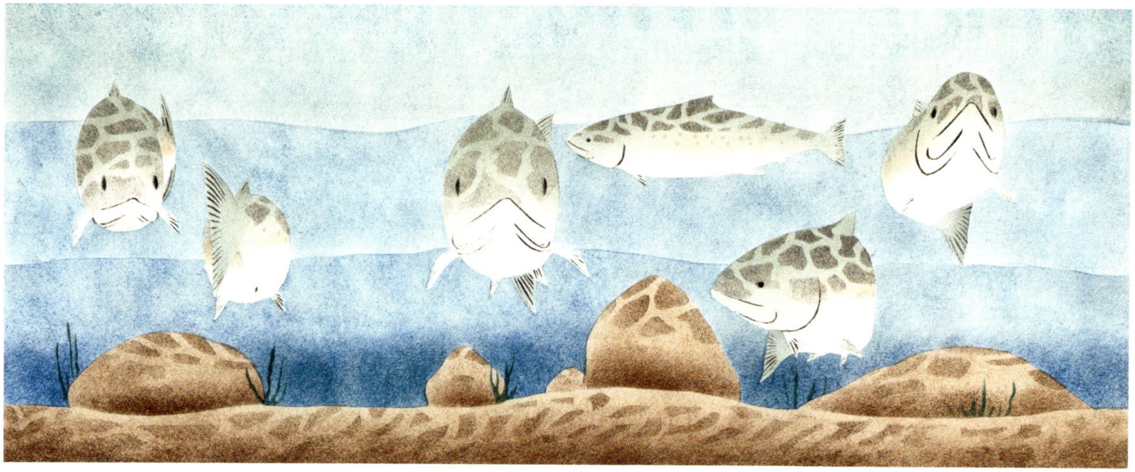

Underwater Char, 1998–#17
Stencil 22/50
28.3 x 63.5
2006-303

Flying, 1998 (uncatalogued)
Stencil 14/75
36.8 x 57.0
2006-364

Shore Birds, 2000–#5
Stencil 24/50
38.0 x 56.3
2006-308

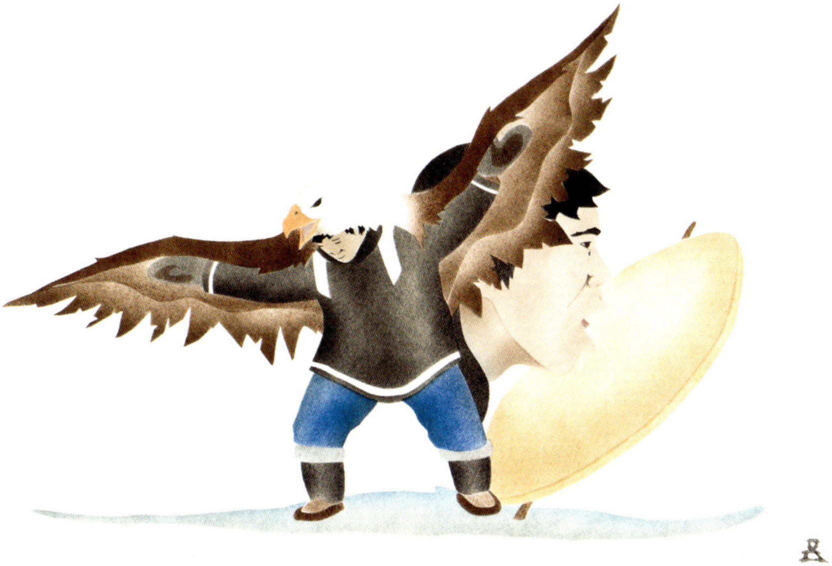

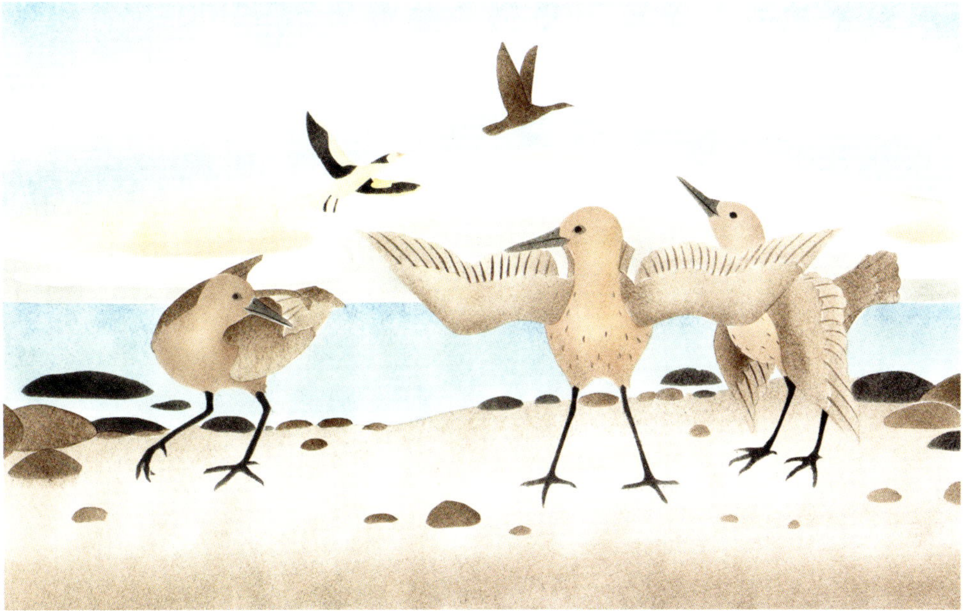

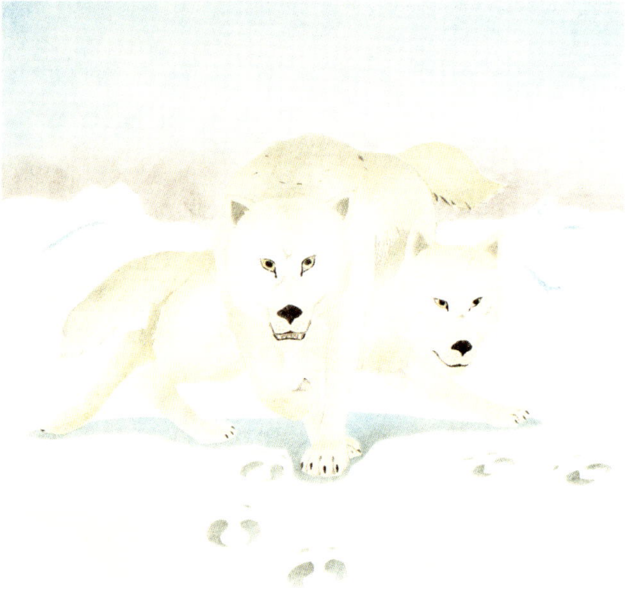

Arctic Wolfs [sic], 2002 (uncatalogued)
Stencil 12/70
44.0 x 43.7
2006-370

Pause, 2003–#18
Stencil 31/70
51.0 x 64.5
2006-323

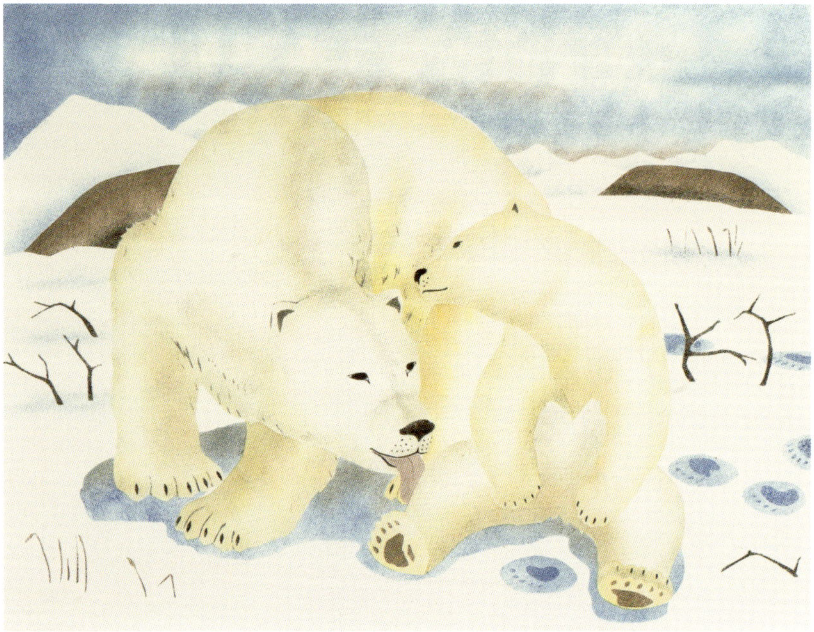

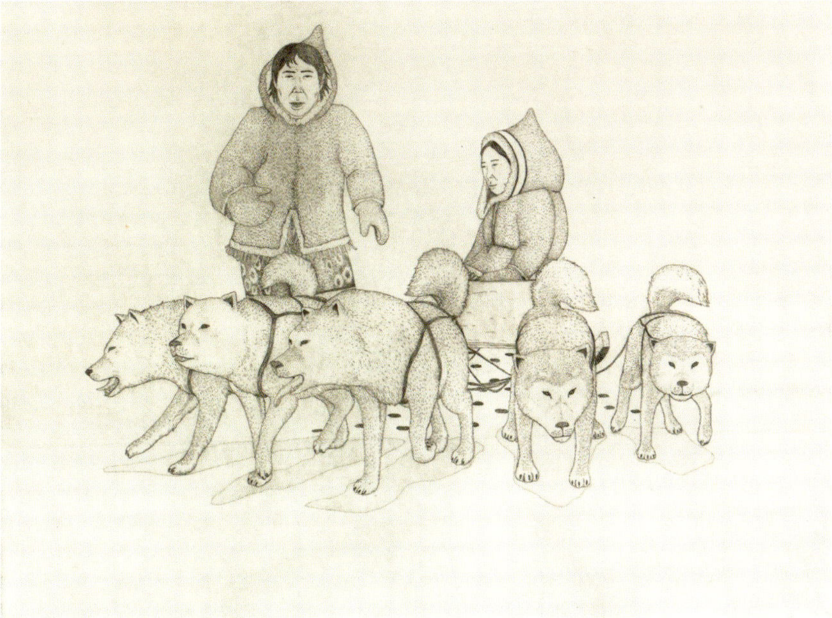

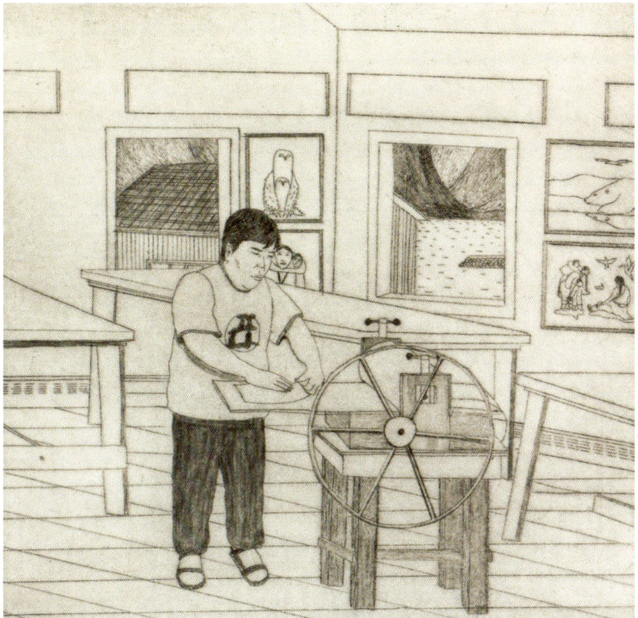

Long Journey Ahead, 2003–#20
Etching 24/70
53.2 x 69.0
2006-325

Andrew Qappik (Self-Portrait in Printshop), 2003–#21
Drypoint Artist Proof IV/V
35.5 x 41.3
2006-326

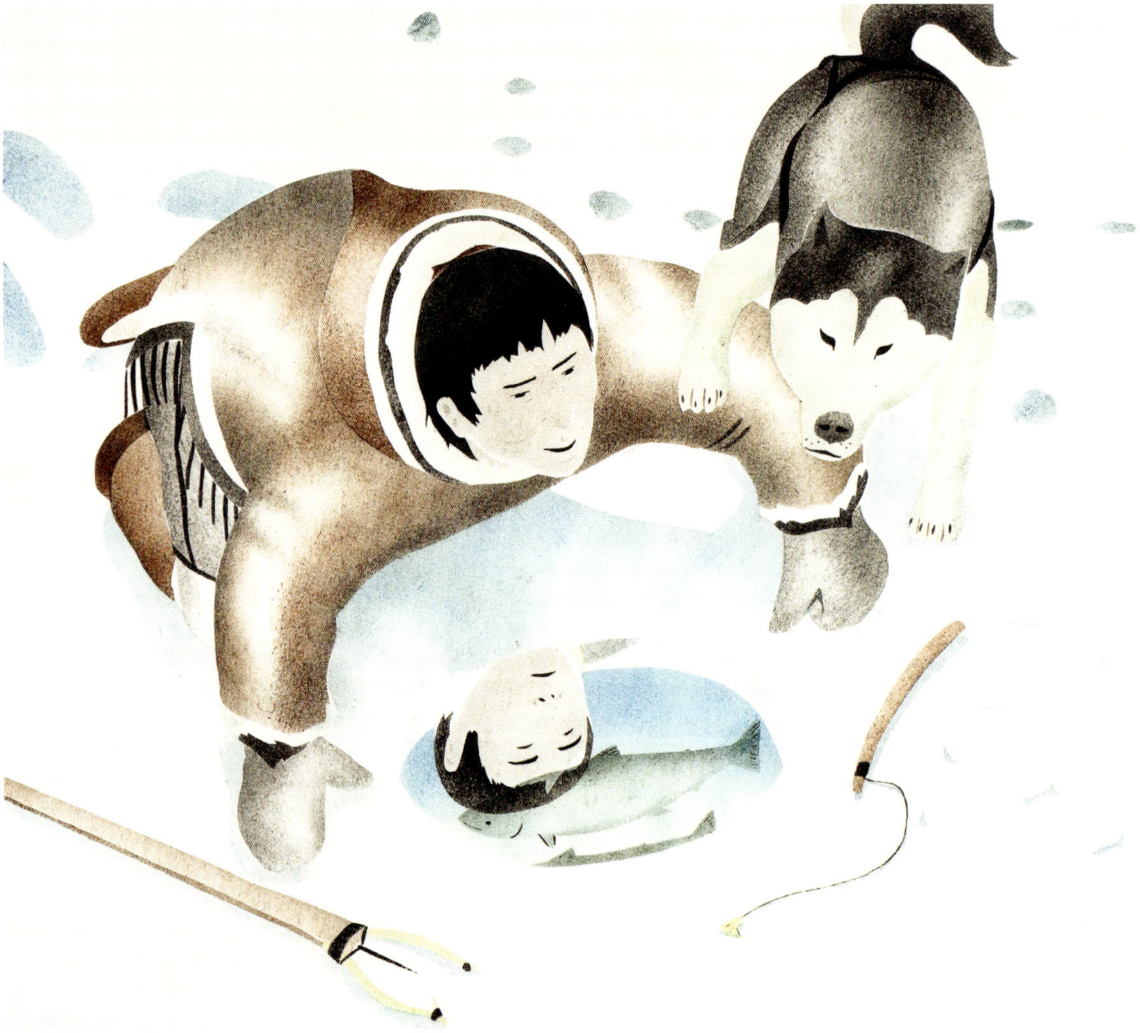

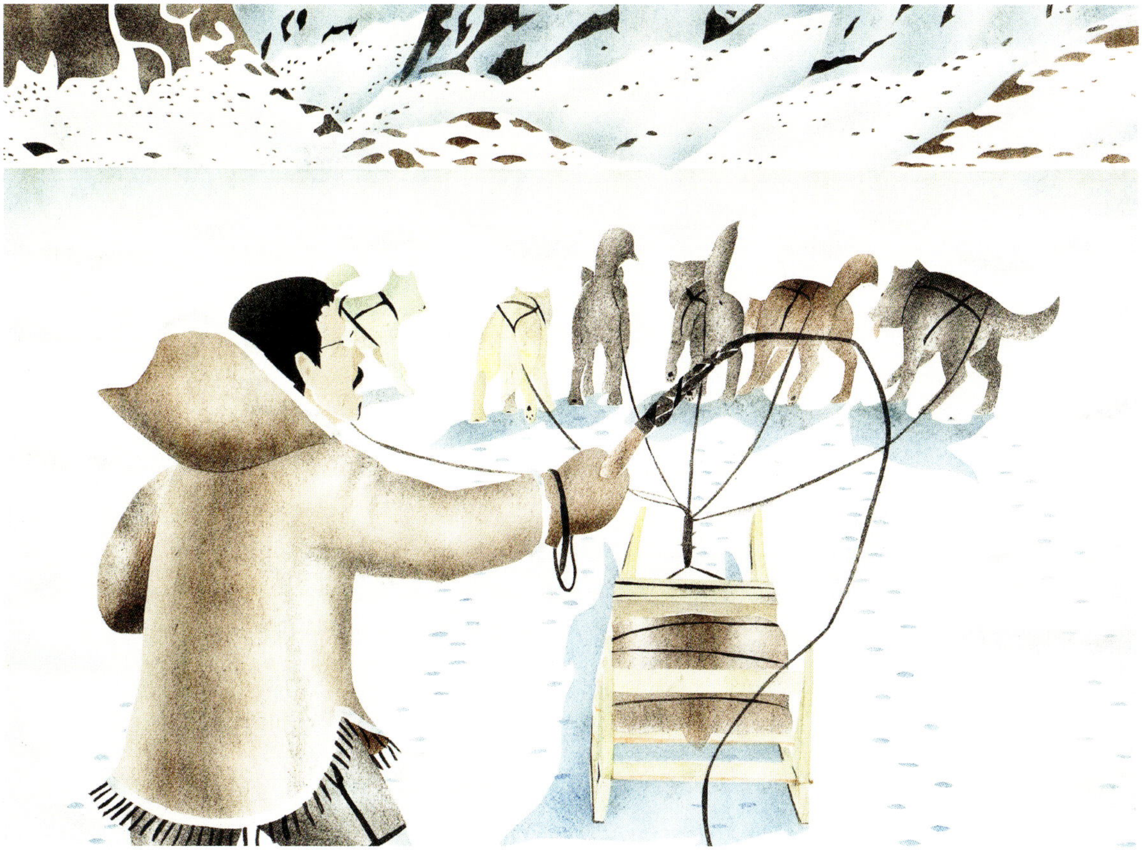

Moment of Appearance, 2004–#24
Stencil 27/50
50.5 x 54.5
2006-327

Driving to Pangnirtung Pass, 2004–#25
Stencil 25/60
50.0 x 63.7
2006-328

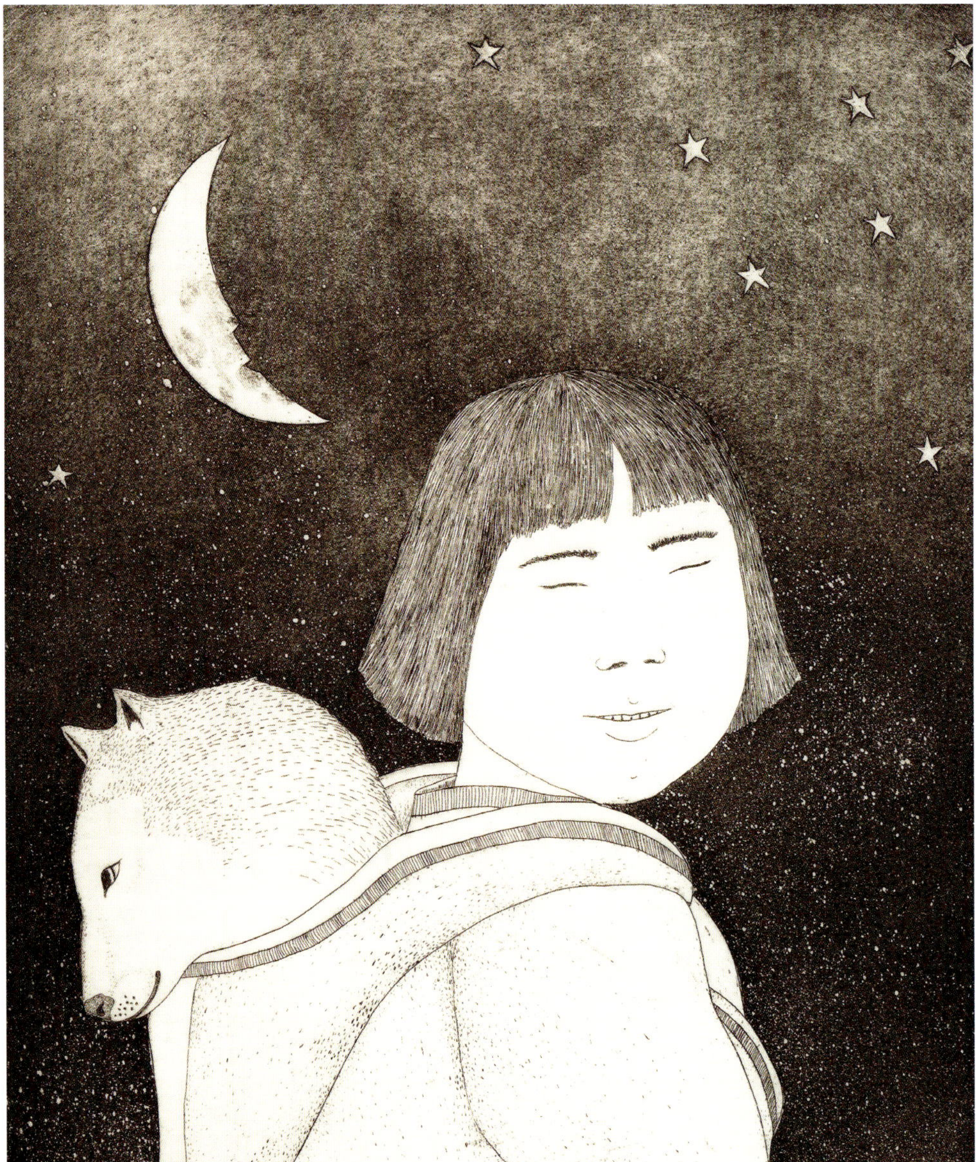

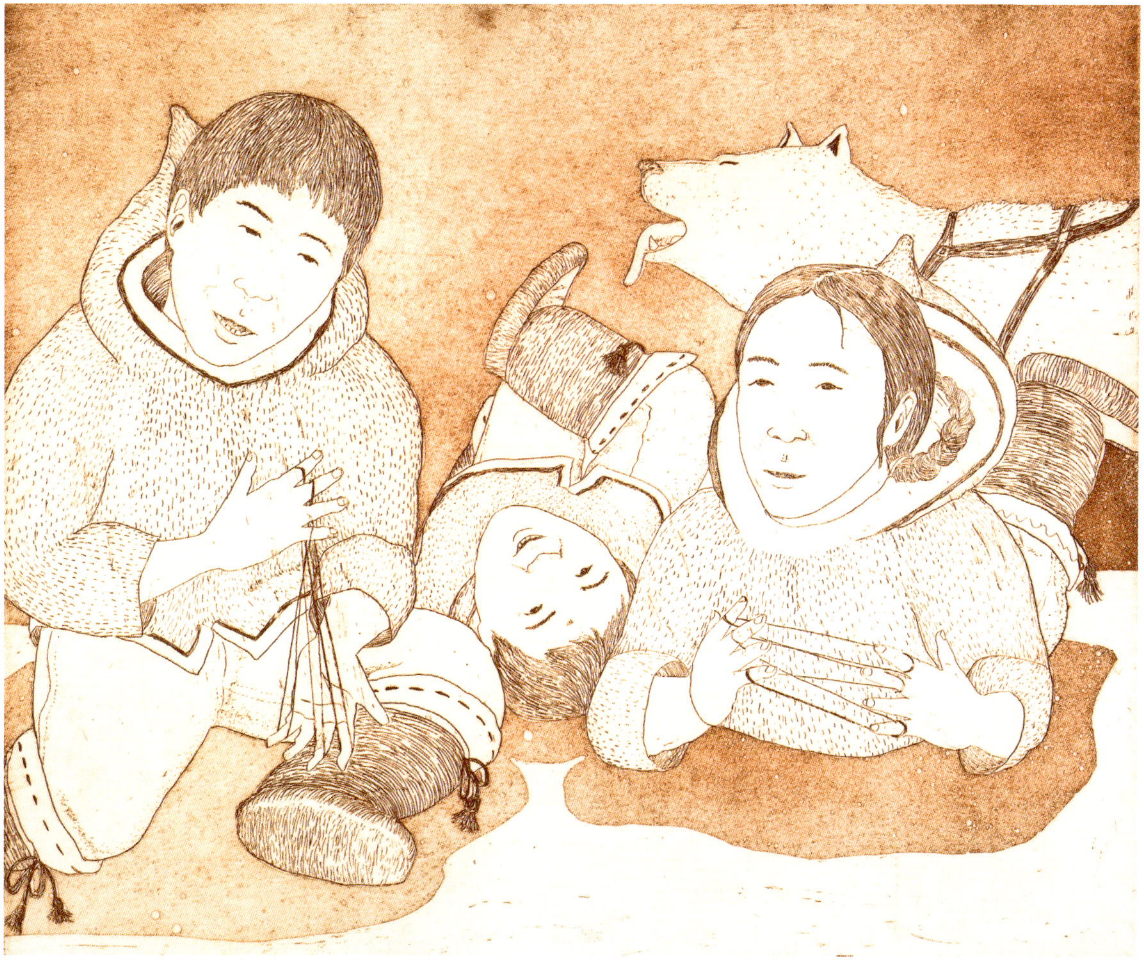

My Daughter Ceporah and Buffy, 2005–#17
Etching 22/35
47.3 x 36.4
2006-331

String Games, 2006–#18
Etching 22/50
33.4 x 38.8
2006-336

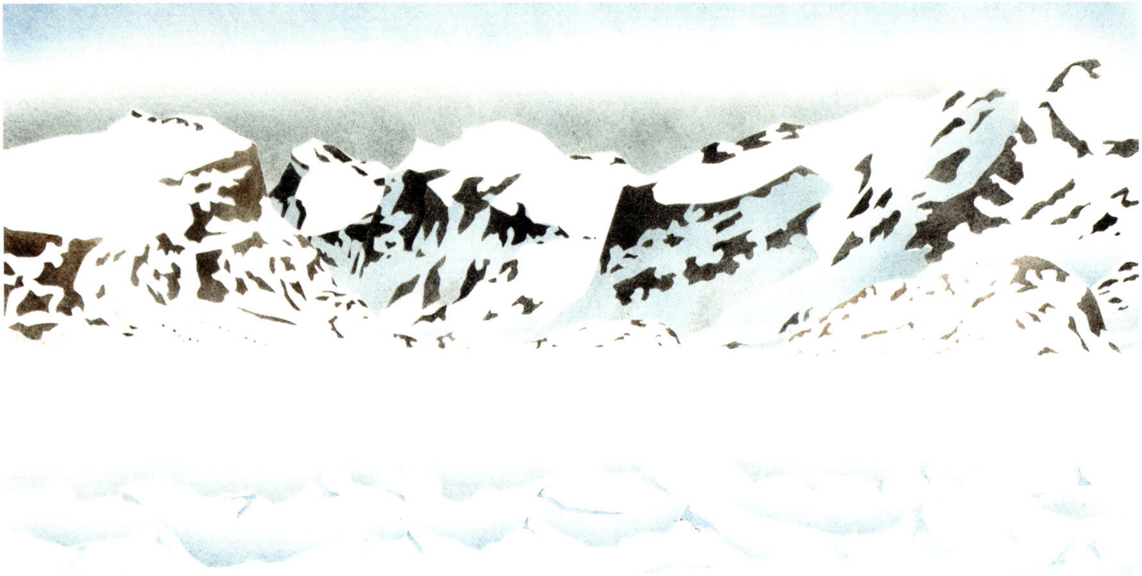

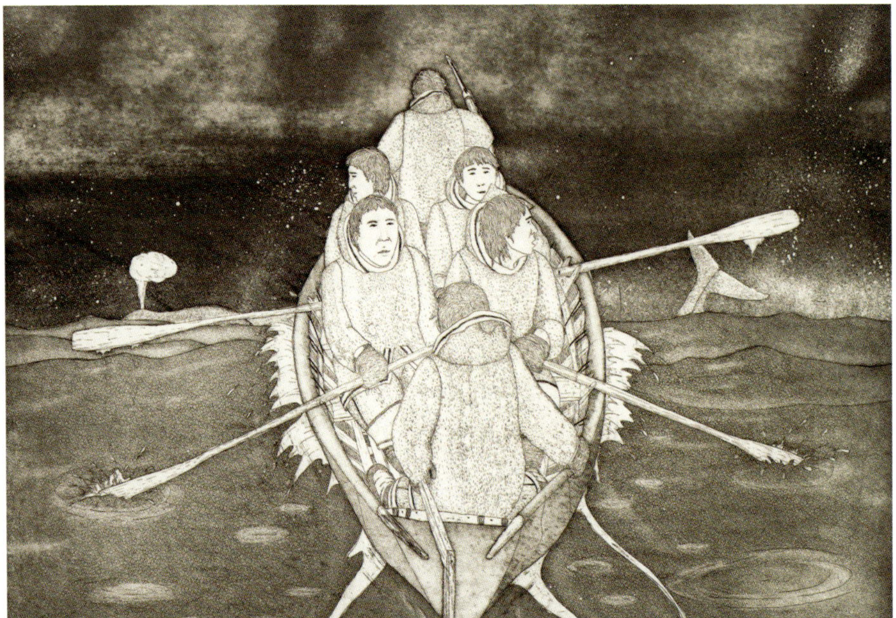

This oil painting was created as the result of a painting workshop held at the Uqqurmiut Centre for Arts and Crafts in Pangnirtung in November 2009. Qappik has created an imagined scene from the time of his grandfathers. His maternal grandfather, Elijah Keenainak and his family lived on the west side of the mountains, on the far shore of the left side of the painting. Keenainak lived and hunted for caribou in an area called Qamakuluit, or "beautiful shelters." In the background of this scene is the spectacular fiord that forms the landscape surrounding the present-day community of Pangnirtung. Today, Qappik's work area in the Uqqurmiut Print Shop looks out on this landscape which is featured in a number of his prints.

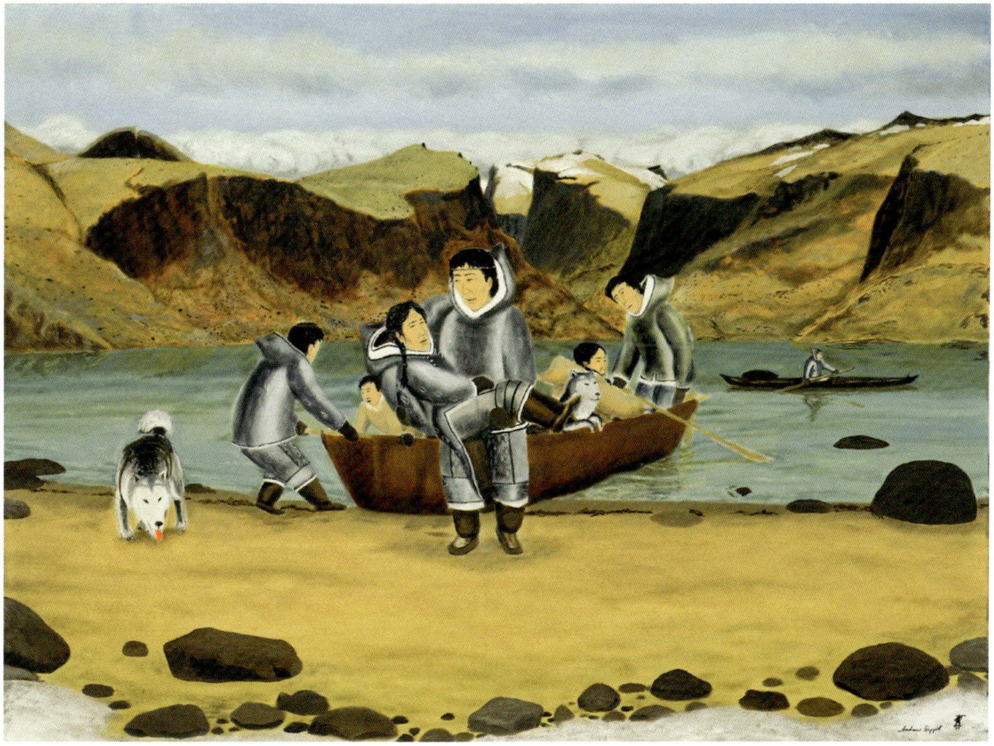

Punniqtuuq (Pangnirtung), 2007–#15
Stencil -28/70
35.0 x 61.0
2007-123

Whales Ahead, 2008–#13
Etching 34/50
53.2 x 67.0
2008-326

People of Pangnirtung, 2009
Oil on canvas
91.5 x 122 cm
2010-25

Bibliography

Fisher, Kyra Vladykov. "Uqqurmiut: New Work by Four Pangnirtung Artists." *Inuit Art Quarterly* 25, no. 1 (Spring 2010) (issue in preparation)

Goetz, Helga. *The Inuit Print/L'estampe inuit*. National Museum of Man, National Museums of Canada, Ottawa, 1977.

Jones, H.G. "Pauloosie Karpik's First Drawings." *Inuit Art Quarterly* 6, no. 3 (Summer 1991): 30–33.

Jones, H.G. *Preserving Inuit Heritage Through Art: The Cataloged Prints of Andrew Qappik, 1978–1998*. H.G. Jones, 1999.

Inuit Art Quarterly. "Pangnirtung Celebrates Re-Opening of Print Shop." 11, no 4 (Winter 1996): 46.

Inuit Art Quarterly. "There were a lot of people who had a say in it." 14, no. 3 (Fall 1999): 48.

McGrath, Robin. "The Influence of Comics on Inuit Art and Literature." *Inuit Art Quarterly* 4, no. 1 (Winter 1989): 4–8.

Pangnirtung print catalogues published as follows:
- Government of the Northwest Territories, 1973
- Pangnirtung Eskimo Co-operative, 1975–1988
- Uqqurmiut Inuit Artists Association, 1992–2008

Pitsiulak, Lipa. "My Ideas Come From Up in the Air," in *Baffin Island*. Winnipeg Art Gallery, Winnipeg, 1983, 11–19.

Rodrigue, Michaela. "From North Carolina to Pangnirtung: art forges lasting bond," *Nunatsiaq News*, July 2, 1999.

Seagrave, Annalisa R. "Regenerations: The Graphic Art of Three Young Artists." *Inuit Art Quarterly* 13, no. 4 (Winter 1998): 4–15.

Thomson, Jane Sproull and Luke Ratzlaff. "Andrew Qappik's Contemporary Arctic Visions." *Inuit Art Quarterly* 20, no. 4 (Winter 2005): 10–16.

Von Finckenstein, Maria, ed. *Nuvisavik: the place where we weave, Inuit tapestries from Arctic Canada*. Gatineau: Canadian Museum of Civilization, 2002.

Pangnirtung Pass, Baffin Island. Photo courtesy of Michael H. Davies.

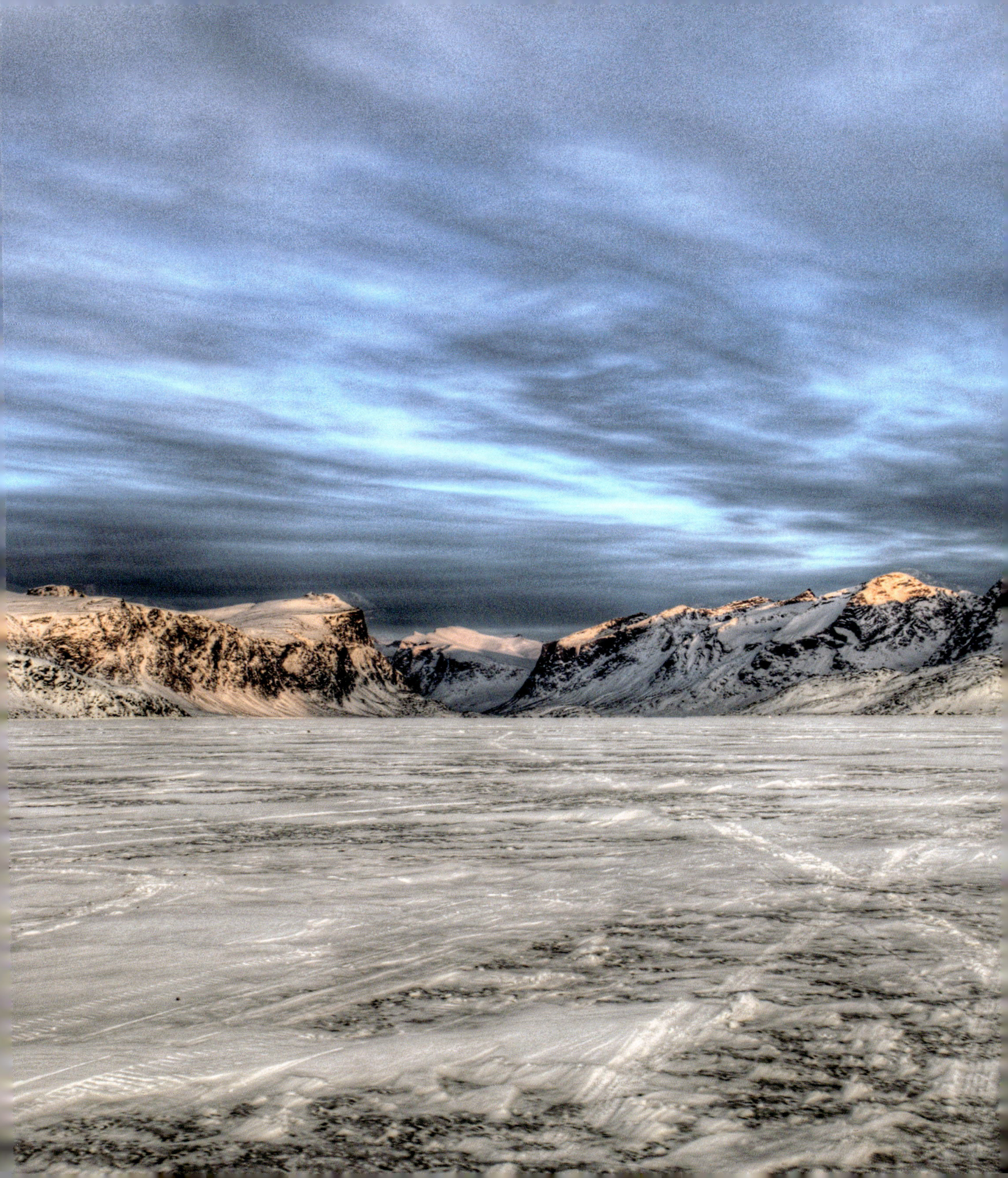